Alice Nolan

The Byrnes of Glengoulah, a True Tale

Alice Nolan

The Byrnes of Glengoulah, a True Tale

ISBN/EAN: 9783337023515

Printed in Europe, USA, Canada, Australia, Japan

Cover: Foto ©Andreas Hilbeck / pixelio.de

More available books at **www.hansebooks.com**

THE

BYRNES OF GLENGOULAH.

A True Tale.

BY

ALICE NOLAN.

NEW YORK:
P. O'SHEA, 27 BARCLAY STREET.

TO THE

FAITHFUL PEOPLE OF IRELAND AND THEIR DESCENDANTS,

SCATTERED OVER EVERY PORTION OF THE HABITABLE GLOBE,

VICTIMS

OF BRITISH RULE AND LANDLORD RAPACITY,

EXILES

FROM OUR OWN BEAUTIFUL AND POETIC LAND, TO WHOSE SOFT VALES AND OCEAN-BOUND SHORES OUR HEARTS EVER FONDLY TURN,

This Tale

IS RESPECTFULLY AND LOVINGLY DEDICATED BY

THE AUTHOR.

PREFACE.

The incidents related in this tale, really and truly occurred, though not in the consecutive order in which they are placed.

The mass of the Irish landlords having attained an unenviable pre-eminence, it was found necessary to concentrate several characters in one individual, and make him the representative of his class: thus the Right-Rev. S. W. Biggs is in reality some superlatively bad landlords exhibiting in one mortal frame. It must not be inferred, however, that the picture is overdrawn, or that there could not be found one person in that class sufficiently wicked to bear the responsibility alone. Unhappily the fact of their being so numerous is the very reason why one must be made to stand for many, otherwise the recital of each individual's inhuman execution of English laws (framed for the destruction of a kindly, virtuous people, and cruel enough to disgrace savages, not to speak of their manifest injustice) would form a library in itself. Another cause also existed, which seemed to render this amalgamation a necessity: The writer was surprised to find that many atrocities perpetrated by landlords within the last twenty-five years were almost unknown in America, even to Irish people who had emigrated before that period; thus the trial and legal murder of Bryan Seery, in Westmeath, had never been heard of by any one with whom the writer conversed in this country during a period of seventeen years! Many other transactions detailed here, which happened under other tyrants, were equally unknown; and although the vast majority of the English-speaking people of the United States are natives of Ireland, or descendants of these persecuted Celts, yet the evictions by Lord Plunket, the Protestant Bishop of Tuam, seem alone to have aroused a cry of indignation throughout this land—thanks to the fearless zeal and energy of dear good Father Lavell, and the saintly, noble Archbishop of Tuam, who would not tamely witness the destruction of their flock. All honor to those Columbkills of the nineteenth century! In view of these facts, it appeared indispensable to collect some of the skeletons of landed proprietors together, thrust them into one wolf's-hide, and hold the disgusting creature up for execration.

After much trouble and correspondence, therefore, the writer obtained a file of the Dublin *Nation* containing a full report of the trial and execution in February, 1846, at the town of Mullingar, County Westmeath, of Bryan Seery, for the murder of Sir Francis Hopkins, Bart., who was not murdered at all, having received a shot through his *hat*, instead of his *heart*, if he ever possessed such a sensitive organ. This noble baronet, then, under the title of one not unknown to the crowbar brigade—Right Reverend Samuel Wilson Biggs, D. D., Lord Bishop of Glengoulah, is the hero, and his deeds, interwoven with others of his class, form the groundwork of this tale.

All the other characters introduced are real. Margin, the agent, is a life likeness, if anything a trifle too flattering. Like all paintings, it conceals many of the blemishes and wrinkles so visible in the original. The names of persons and places are changed for obvious reasons.

The record of the O'Byrne family, as related by Mr. De Courcy to Biggs, is not their history. It is merely a fancy sketch. The O'Byrnes have, indeed, a truly noble history, but its details are too long for the pages of such a tale as the present.

Having said so much by way of explanation, it only remains to crave the indulgence of the reader for the author, who is perfectly sensible of the literary demerits of the undertaking, it having been originally written during invalid hours for dear young relatives, who never saw the old historic land of their fathers.

THE BYRNES OF GLENGOULAH.

CHAPTER I.

DEAR READER, have you ever been in the beautiful County of Wicklow, in Ireland? I pity you if you have not, and will pity you still more if, having the means, you do not visit before you die that land of enchanting scenery—for Moore tells us (and I think you will admit he is pretty good authority),

> "There is not in this wide world a valley so sweet
> As that vale in whose bosom the bright waters meet."

That vale is the Vale of Ovoca, so called from a stream of liquid silver bearing the same name, which takes its rise in the neighboring hills, bounds from cliff to cliff into the lovely valley below, where, meeting the limpid Avon, they clasp each other in a bright and gurgling embrace. Soon disengaging itself, the Ovoca dashes forward, singing and tumbling as it runs through the picturesque village of "Wooden Bridge," then turning the little headland it seems to expand its bosom and move more slowly —no doubt out of courtesy to the honors paid it in flowing through the groves of Shelton, where the sweeping willow and the graceful larch bend their branches to kiss the beautiful stream as it passes. Emerging from those lovely shades it makes a curve by the lighthouse of Arklow, and with a joyous bound flings itself into the arms of "the Irish Sea, or St. George's Channel," which forms the eastern boundary of Ireland. Oh, happy, cloudless days of childhood! How vividly ye impress the memory! Many a sunny morning in summer have I wandered in those enchanted groves, with—a book you will think, of course; nothing of the kind—a goodly-sized basket on my arm, and a pair of scissors contained therein; for, reader, my taste was not of the literary kind then, I assure you—to pick blackberries, or hunt for bird's nests, was then the bent of my inclination. Armed, therefore, with the basket and scissors aforesaid (the latter was to save our hands from the swarms of little thorns which guarded the fruit), my sister and self committed great depredations on the blackberries (which, by the way, were the largest and most luscious of the kind I have ever tasted). Often has my sister—who was ever more piously inclined than I was—called to me from a neighboring bush to stop and recite the "Angelus," as, clear as the morning air, broke the tones of Shelton Abbey bell for six o'clock; not, as of old, to call the faithful to prayer, but to summon the laborers to work on the estate of the Right-Hon. the Earl of Wicklow, whose magnificent country seat lay on the opposite side of the river. I see it all before me now, though more than thirty years have gone by—the clear, bright, sunny morning, the ever-verdant grass dotted with myriads of daisies and cowslips, the gentle kine moving slowly and browsing the sweet herbage, groups of sheep with tiny lambs nibbling or playing on the turf; the gurgling limpid river "murmuring a happy song" as it glides on to the sea, the graceful trees along its banks bending to catch the reflection of their own fair forms on its bosom, the hills of Shelton at one side of the river and Castle Howard on the other, rising cone after cone, clothed to the very top with every variety of tree and shrub. To the east a break in the hills discloses the slender minarets and turrets of Shelton Abbey towering from the distant groves; more distant still, the pretty little town of Arklow, with its long line of fishermen's huts stretching out to the beach; and, still beyond, the blue sea with its tiny crests of foam and mimic waves, scarcely rocking the little fishing-smacks, with which it is now covered, bent on their daily toil. The air is redolent with the perfume of wild-flowers. From every bush and brake thousands upon thousands of birds are pouring forth their joyous songs, and high in the heavens numberless larks are taking their melodious way—

> " Who, singing ever soar,
> And soaring ever sing."

Two children have stopped their blackberry feast to recite, in union with the whole Catholic world, the beautiful "Angelus Domini." Their garb is black, for a few months before the loved voice that taught them that sweet Christian practice had ceased to be heard on earth! Well! Pardon me, reader, when I found myself on the banks of the Ovoca I could not for my life but try to paint, however imperfectly, the beautiful panorama which memory conjured up; but now we will let it move on, and I will proceed to tell you my tale.

About four miles from this lovely scene, at the base of one of those cone-shaped hills, was a snug farm of about forty acres, held by one Anthony Byrne, as decent a man and as honest a neighbor as ever the sun shone on. Anthony, or, as he was usually called, Toney Byrne, arose with the lark, and like that bird of melody went to his work with a light heart, singing or whistling some sweet old melody of his native land, his "fack" on his shoulder, and his two stout farm-laborers bent in the same direction. Like the great majority of Irish peasants Toney Byrne led a blameless life. If he met a neighbor going to work, or returning from it, some such conversation would be sure to ensue as the following: "God save you, Toney!" "Oh, God save you, kindly, Ned! how are you the mornin'?" "Why, then, the Lord be praised, I was never better in my life; and how are you, and how is the woman that owns you?"

"We're all pretty lively, thanks be to the great God, and to you for askin'." "How is the crops wid you, Toney?"

"Well, finely; thanks be to God!" or as the case might be. "Why, then—indeed, Ned, they're mighty backward this season, the Lord of heaven be praised! The upland hay turned out very short entirely, and I'm greatly afeard of the oats too—but sure we can't expect things to be always goin' right; bedad I'm thinkin' we'd have ne'er a thought at all for th' other world if we didn't meet some little disappointment here, so we must only be satisfied when we know we did our best."

"Throth its true for you, Toney; I'm in dread my

whate will be short too; but as you say, when we did our part we can't help it, so welkim be the will of God."

Every one who knows anything of the Irish peasantry knows how common such dialogues are in every part of Ireland. The leading characteristics of the people are gratitude to God in prosperity or adversity, and humble submission to the Divine will under all trials and circumstances.

At the conclusion of their frugal supper Toney and his family would give hearty thanks to God in the real old Catholic fashion, never forgetting to pray for the souls of the faithful departed. After supper all would gather around the bright turf fire to tell stories and crack jokes while the pipe was handed about.

If a stranger happened to be present, which was very often the case (for Toney Byrne, like a true Irishman, never closed his door to the poor or the stranger), he got the snuggest seat in the ample chimney corner; then some of the neighbors would raise the latch and step in with "God save all here!" "God save you kindly, and you're welcome; sit down."

"Faix, Barney," one of the youngsters would cry out, "you forgot to say barrin the cat and the dog."

"Sorra matter avic! let the poor brutes have pace; you oughtn't to be so hard on the animals anyhow, Mike."

This sent the laugh round at Mike's expense, a young urchin of ten, who crept grinning up to his father's side on the hearth. I know of no place where a more social evening can be spent than in the kitchen of an Irish peasant farmer. Thrilling ghost stories, poetic fairy tales, and very frequently dissertations and arguments on history, for the Irish peasant is very fond of, and not at all ignorant of, historic lore.

Napoleon le Grand is his great hero, principally because the English hated him; and after detailing and discussing his various exploits, you are sure to hear, "Aye, Boney was able for them all, and would bate the whole world if he let the Pope alone." There every one chimes in, and all are unanimous in pointing out how his power waned from the hour he meddled with the Holy Father, and how just it was he should die in exile as he caused the Sovereign Pontiff to die in a foreign land in his old age. Thus many a pleasant hour passed, and when bed-time came the neighbors, wishing a kindly "good night," would retire to their homes. Then Toney and his bustling, good-natured little wife, calling the household together, would pull out the beads and recite the rosary before lying down to rest.

A couple of times in the year the townlands of Glengoulah were visited in turn by Darby Wholahan, the blind piper, who drew melodious strains from a very respectable-looking, silver-keyed instrument, which he called the "Union Pipes," and which was a combination of the Scotch and Irish bagpipe. The most staid fool in the parish could not keep still while Darby performed the "Peeler's Cap," or "Lord Macdonald's Reel;" and as for "The Hunter's Jig," you'd give your oath you heard the fox running for his life, and the hounds in full cry after him.

Darby was kept going from one farm-house to another, all the neighbors assembling each evening where he was known to be, and the Terpsichorean performances on every floor were a triumph of grace and agility. Between the pauses in the dance Darby had an inexhaustible fund of anecdotes replete with humor; he could, besides, sing an excellent song, either comic or sentimental, and had a great talent for recitation, so that it is no wonder every hand was extended and every heart bounded when Darby arrived. "Oh, God be with those happy days! Oh, God be with my childhood!

Every meeting passed off pleasantly and innocently, and each arose next morning refreshed for the day's work by the harmless and healthful recreation of the evening before.

Thus passed the even tenor of Toney's life and his neighbors. They were not rich in this world's goods, but they wanted for nothing, having wherewithal to live upon, and enough besides to share with their poorer fellow-creatures—a little store maybe for cases of emergency, and immense treasures in Faith, Hope, and Charity. No doubt they had their faults too—who has not? but they were few, and so overlaid with virtues that they could scarcely be perceived.

The landlord who owned this fine estate was Sir Charles Plover, Bart. He was an absentee, and his property was managed with justness and kindness by Mr. De Courcey, a wealthy merchant who had extensive flour mills not far distant. Mr. De Courcey watched over the interests of the tenantry like a wise and prudent man, knowing that the real interest of the landlord was in the prosperity of the tenant. He had the best farm seeds brought from Dublin for their use, saw that their fields were properly drained, encouraged them to keep their houses neat and to train some creeping vine around them, for which purpose he made presents to the farmers' wives and daughters of many a honeysuckle and woodbine.

He had hedges planted here, overtopping banks removed there, mountain rills widened and made to form water-courses for the use of the cattle and to carry off field drains, obliged them to sink wells, and all to have neat and well-kept gates and cattle-pens. By a properly-arranged mixture of justice, firmness and prudence, he made Sir Charles Plover's estate the most prosperous both for landlord and tenant in the county of Wicklow, while the eye of the tourist was enraptured with the scene of tranquil beauty. On the sides of the hills the white farm-houses gleamed from clumps of trees, trailing vines of the sweet-scented honeysuckle crept around the windows and rustic porch, the blue smoke curled high up in the air, the little vegetable garden with here and there a bed of cultivated flowers bordered with "London Pride" formed a bright patch, and helped the primroses to scent the mountain breeze.

Mr. De Courcey was not a Catholic, but he was a gentleman, and presumed not to interfere with the faith of the tenantry. He respected those who lived up to the dictates of their consciences, and was often heard to speak in terms of high admiration of the noble fidelity with which the Catholics of Ireland clung to their faith through weal or woe.

To say that Mr. De Courcey was respected and beloved by the tenants would be cold words; he was almost idolized. Second only in their affections to the venerable Father Esmond, and his curate Father O'Toole, was the much-loved agent. His appearance amongst them ever brought a smile of welcome, while each busied him or herself to appear their best before " Mr. De Courcey, God bless him."

What a pity that the fair face of nature should ever be overcast by a cloud; but clouds and storms will come, dear reader, and so, taking a sheltered seat before it breaks upon us, and keeping our eyes fixed on God's good Providence, "who rules the whirlwind and directs the storm," we will rest awhile and leave the outburst for another chapter.

CHAPTER II.

BEFORE I proceed further I must tell you about Toney's family—as likely a set of children as you could meet with—two girls and three boys. Margaret, the eldest, was a hard-working, gentle-tempered girl, unobtrusively industrious, ever at hand when her mother wanted her, which was pretty nearly the whole day, for Mrs. Byrne was of a bustling, quick-tempered nature, but had the warmest and kindest heart in the world. Margaret was a tall, well-proportioned girl, with an open, smiling face, and the bloom of youth and health on her cheek. She was about 18 at the time my tale commences. Winifred, who was not yet 14, was a smaller figure, with a remarkably pretty face, in which drollery and roguery were the leading characteristics. She was a great pet with her father, who would shield her from her mother's anger when some piece of work allotted to her would be found untouched, or when she had played some prank on the old schoolmaster who came to teach them three evenings in the week. "Whist, Kitty," he would say, "the girl is young; and if she is fond of playing tricks, the creature has no more harm in them nor a kitten." So Winnie went on playing pranks and laughing merrily. But the darling of his mother's heart was Andrew, the eldest boy, now about 12; he resembled his father in figure, being remarkably tall for his age; while his features were like his mother's, fair and frolicsome. He bore a strong resemblance to his sister Winnie, and was ever ready to second her in all her pranks; but there was no son more docile or obedient than Andy, for all his devil-may-care ways and hasty temper. One day, when speaking confidentially of her family to a neighbor who had dropped in, Mrs. Byrne was known to say, "Margie and little Pat is the father on the sod—there's no trouble in life wid them,— they go smooth along, gainin' the good-will of everybody; deed, Mrs. Fehily, though I'm her mother, I will say Margie is worth her weight in gold; you could not cross her temper; but for all she has a dacent spirit too—there's not a mane thought nor a mane act in her carcass." "Mane!" cried Mrs. Fehily; "why, then, I'd like to know where anything mane could be got in the Byrnes of Glengoulah! Sure we wouldn't know where to go look for dacency if we didn't find it in the ould stock."

"I'm beholdin' to you, Mrs. Fehily, for your good word; but, indeed, it's true what you say. Sure everybody knows the Byrnes is the oldest family in Wicklow, barrin the O'Tools, and though I know myself Toney is proud of them too. Still he's always tellin' the children the way to prove they're of the ould stock is to be good, humble Christians, and to never forget how the Byrnes of ancient times was hung, drawn, and quartered for bein' Catholics, but they kept their faith through thick and thin, though they lost their lands."

"'Deed, Mrs. Byrne, it's often I heard my grandfather tellin' of all the hardships they met with from Crom'ell and his crew; bad luck to their memories, the black-hearted villains!"

"Well, may God in his mercy keep the persecution from our doors anyway; but I was tellin' you about the children. If Margie and Pat is like the Byrnes, there's Winnie and Andy and Mike has the very spirit of the Malones—my own people."

"Why, then, now, do you tell me so?"

"Tell you so! Two apples never grew more like one another than my Andy and his uncle—my poor brother, Andy Malone—that I christened him after; God rest his soul this day! Oh, Mrs. Fehily, dear! if you were to see that boy when he was risin' twenty-two!—there wasn't the match of him in three baronies. He was as tall and straight as an arrow—the Malones was all tall and likely, glory be to God; it's after the Delanys, my mother's people, I take in my height. Well, he had a pair of shoulders on him the breadth of your apron, and sorra such a lad for tricks in the country round. He'd sing like a lark the minit he'd open his eye in the mornin'; and it's tryin' the steps in a double or a reel he'd be while he'd be puttin' on him (dressing); then he'd kneel down and pray—I'll engage as fervent as any one—and be off to his work; but when breakfast time came maybe we wouldn't all get our share. Before he'd go to the field again he'd put myself and Onny and Mary and Biddy (there was the four sisters of us growing up) all in a heap a top of one another on the floor, and the spinnin' wheel a top of us again. My mother used to run after him, makin' believe she was goin' to hit him a box, and he'd whisk her up in his arms, and run round and round the house with her, and then put her sittin' in her own chair in the chimbley corner and run off. We couldn't do a ha'porth but laughin' for an hour after, and my poor mother holdin' her sides. He was as innocent as a child, for he'd stay a whole day, when it would be too wet to work, playin' wid little Norah and

Tommy, and makin' babby houses for them, and then he'd dance for the creatures. Oh, dear! oh, dear! glory be to the holy God! but it's hard to live in this world at all." Here poor Mrs. Byrne, overcome by her feelings, rocked back and forth and sobbed in her apron, upon which Mrs. Fehily inquired what happened him? "Happened him! They broke his heart, so they did. Didn't ould Wilson, the tithe proctor, come to take up the tithes one day, and my mother and himself had some words and he gave her the lie? Andy was just comin' in at the door on the minit when he heard the word; and, Mrs. Fehily, dear, it would do your heart good to see him leapin' on Wilson. Well, he bate him and kicked him till he cried for mercy. 'Now,' says he, 'I'll tache you how to spake to a dacent woman,' says he, 'you blood-suckin' varmint that's livin' by the plunder of the honest and the hard workin' poor, yourself and your employers,' says he; 'be out of the house this minit, or I'll have your life,' says he. Wilson was glad enough to get leave to go; but before evenin' fell a whole possee of polis came and took my poor fellow away to prison. Och! Mrs. Fehily, asthore! but that was the black night in our house; the neighbors had to hold my father when he seen the polis puttin' handcuffs on his darlin' boy; my poor mother fell off in a dead faint when she seen the polis comin' in, and well become my poor fellow but he tried to comfort the father. 'Never mind, father dear,' says he, 'it won't be for long; I'll soon be back again wid you all, plaze God,' says he. He was going to say more, but they dragged him off. He was four months in prison before the trial came on, although the best of bail was offered for him—they said it was too great a crime to bate a tithe proctor, and they could not think of taking bail for it. When the trial came on you'd think he was the greatest villain that ever lived to hear the charges brought against him—it would frighten you to hear the papers read by the prosecutin' counsil; they said he was a dangerous character and must be made an example of. And when they said, 'stand up, Andrew Malone, and plead guilty or not guilty to these charges,' he stood up as grand as an earl. 'If you mane,' says he, 'am I guilty of baitin' and kickin' the tithe proctor?—*I am*,' says he; 'I gave him as good a kickin' as ever he got, and the man doesn't live that I'd let give the lie to any dacent woman, let alone my own mother. I hope Wilson wont forget the lesson I gave him in good manners,' says he. He was as brave as a lion and didn't care a fiv'penny bit for the whole of them. A wild cheer and cries of 'bravo, Andy Malone!' rung through the court. The Judge, mighty angry, called for silence, and said if they done that any more he would have the court cleared. They then told my poor fellow to sit down and would not let him say another word, though he had no counsil; he would not let my father fee counsil, for he said it would be of no use, and sure it was true for him. They then sentenced him to twelve months' imprisonment and hard labor. Och! but it was the sore year to us goin' in and out of prison tryin' to bring him the little comforts he was used to. Many's the fine turkey and pair of barn doors (fat fowl) we brought the jailor to get his good will for Andy, but he was trated nothing the better for it. He didn't care for the work, for he was as strong as a horse; but they put him with the riff raff of the prison on purpose to break his spirit, and well they did it. When that weary year was out and he was let out you wouldn't know him. He tried to laugh and joke as of old to comfort the mother, but *she* could not be deceived—she saw the change in him, and the light went out from her heart from that hour. The damp of the prison cell got into his bones; and the close confinement, but above all the keepin' company with house-breakers and horse-thieves, broke his heart. His cheek was pale and his step was heavy, and he faded and faded, and before the harvest was all in he hadn't a bit on his bones and had to keep his bed; and by the end of October, when the laves was all fallin' in showers, and the wind was moanin' through the deserted branches, we follied him to his grave;—the strong and the brave was low in his youth."* Here poor Mrs. Byrne, throwing her apron over her head and rocking to and fro, gave way to a burst of grief. The sympathizing Mrs. Fehily, who was weeping too, exclaimed indignantly, "Och! then I pray this day that the vengeance of————"

"Oh stop, Mrs. Fehily, dear! Whist asthore—don't curse them! He bid us not with his dyin' breath. Mother darlin', says he, the heart in my body

---

* A similar case occurred in Carlow in (I think) 1832 or 1833. Two respectable farmers, brothers, who held land under a landlord named Watson, exercised their newly-acquired franchise by voting for the liberal candidate. The landlord was enraged, and shortly after indicted them for maiming two horses, his property. They were lodged in jail—all bail refused; and by some quibble of law their trial was postponed from one assizes to another until they lay a whole year in prison. At length they were brought to trial, and the principal evidence against them was a woman whose character was so notoriously bad that there was a burst of indignation through the court when she was put upon the witness stand. The prisoners' counsel, on her cross-examination, made her contradict herself three times. The prosecuting counsel ordered her to retire, and the men were acquitted. The younger brother, a high-spirited young man, was so grieved by the associations to which they were exposed, and the hardships of prison life, that he sank rapidly and died in a few weeks after his release! The witness, whose name was Anne Magee, her brother, and other members of her family, had free quarters in Dublin Castle for years, and were regular informers for the Crown. The present writer has frequently seen her with a brace of pistols in her belt, and report said that she carried a dagger in her bosom.

was broke when they put me in with thieves and murderers; and when I thought how no one belong in' to me was ever so disgraced before, I made up my mind one night in the cold cell not to bear it if I was to be hung for it; and when we were turned into the yard next mornin', says he, who should be waitin' to see me but Father Delany—God lave him his health! Well I up and told him what was in my mind, and he put his hand on my head and said—mother, I'll never forget his words—My poor child! says Father Delany, says he, I know you since the day you were christened, and I knew your father and mother before you, and its a great trial upon the son of virtuous parents; but Andy asthore, says he, don't you know who was put between two thieves and crucified in the presence of His Blessed Mother?—it was the Lord of all glory, my dear son, and he suffered it for your sake, to teach you patience and humility. Bear everything then manfully for His sake who bore so much for yours, and He will give you a crown of glory and the company of the blessed saints and angels forever. It was then, mother, that he took the silver crucifix from his own neck and put it on mine, and told me often to look at it and think on our blessed Lord's sufferins; and, mother darlin', I got quite calm and changed ever since—'deed I'm thinkin' it's obliged to them I ought to be that I'm goin' young from this world and its hardships. Sure, mother darlin', this life is short and very cold, says he, and we will be all soon together, where we will never see sorra any more. And, mother jewel, says he, don't let any one belongin' to me curse them that brought me low in my youth, for the Lord of glory on the blessed cross prayed for them that nailed him to it; and Father Delany says it's His will that I'm goin'—och! och! Mrs. Fehily, dear, it would break your heart if you were to hear him talkin' like a bishop for all the world. My poor mother would say to all, "yes, avic machree! sure it's the truth you're spakin', darlin' of my heart."

She never left him night nor day; and when he was gone she was like one stupified.

The day of the berrin' she took a tremlin' all over, and we wanted her not to go, but she said she'd stay by him while ever he'd be above ground. When they were fillin' up the grave she stood by, and while my father and the rest of us, even to the neighbors, were cryin' like the rain, she never shed a tear, but, risin' her hands and eyes to Heaven, she said—in a voice that pierced the hearts of all present, for it was mournful as the cry of a banshee—"May God and His Blessed Mother receive your soul this day, my darlin' fair-haired boy—the joy of my life and the light of my eyes—I'm a sorrowful, broken-hearted woman now." She took the tremblin' again. We brought her home and put her to bed, and she never 'riz from it!—that day six weeks we laid her by the side of Andy. Och! but ours was the cold, black house, where there used to be nothin' but singin' and laughin' the live long day. My poor father struggled the best he could for a year and a half, but the faver broke out—God bless the hearers—(here both women made the sign of the cross on their foreheads)—and he took it, and by rason of his bein' broke down by his great troubles he couldn' stand it, so we buried him too. And little Tommy and Norah—tho creatures sickened and died the week after my father—we always thought Andy and my mother done that by their prayers before the weeny little ones knew what hardship was. "Oh, God! rest all their souls in glory this day, Amen!" Oh, Amen, amen! Mrs. Byrne, dear! —but glory be to God! Sure if you had your share of trouble in your young days, God is makin' up to you now for it! Oh, praises be to His holy name! It's true what you say, Mrs. Fehily; asthore it was my luck to get one of the quietest men in the seven parishes, and the most industrious. Then I have good bidable children, thanks be to God; and my sisters is all married comfortable;—so, as you say, Mrs. Fehily, God is makin' up to me sure enough for the troubles of my youth, and it's a great deal more than I deserve." The distant sound of Shelton Abbey bell, ringing for the laborers to leave off work, warned Mrs. Fehily that supper-time was coming. Hastily picking up her ball of worsted which rolled upon the floor, and sticking her needles in the stocking she was knitting, she wished Mrs. Byrne a good evening, ran across the road, and mounting the stile crossed into the neighboring field, where she met her husband and two sons returning from work, and they all trudged home together.

CHAPTER III.

A SHORT time after the conversation detailed in the last chapter, one fine Sunday, Toney Byrne and his family were coming down the hill after hearing mass in Glengoulah chapel, when they were overtaken by Ned Fehily and family. After the usual greetings, commenting on the sermon delivered by Father O'Toole, etc., etc., Toney asked Ned to let the women and children walk on, and to come with him and see the oat-field. So they crossed the ditch through an opening in the hawthorn and went over the farm.

But few words had passed between them when Ned asked, "Why, then, Toney, is it true what I hear that you're goin' to get your little girl marrid?" "Well, 'deed I dun know yet, Ned; she's speakin' to a boy of the Donohoes of Cool-a-glisson, in the county Wexford, and the mother is mighty partial to the match, but I didn't give in yet." "And why not, Toney? Sure I know Bartle Donohoe well, and a clane likely boy he is, and more betoken the child of as dacent a father and mother as any in the same county, though I know he's no match for one of the Byrnes if things was as they ought." "Oh! be dad, the sorra fault I have to find with him on that score, oh no! I have a mighty great regard, indade, for the same boy; and sure Father Esmond tells me he got a great account of him entirely from his own parish priest. It isn't that at all; but you see, Ned, I have to look into the well-bein' of my little girl; and what I don't like is this: You see Tom Donohoe has four other boys besides Bartle, and I belave three daughters; and though he has a fine well-stocked farm, and holds under Earl Fitzwilliam—one of the best landlords in Ireland—still and all if he goes to divide up his farm between the boys it will leave each of them only a strugglin' livelihood, and I think Margie can do better than that; the colleen is young, and has plenty of time before her. So I told Bartle my mind a fortnight ago, and he agreed to wait awhile and see if some arrangement could be made. He came to tell me, a few days ago, he heard a report that Pat Hanlon of Moyglish is talkin' of goin' to America. Pat has an uncle in Canada that's goin' to leave him a power of money, and he speaks of goin' out to him with his wife and child—you know he has but the one little slip of a girl—and in case he does go, he'll be givin' up his farm; so Bartle set off a Friday to see the earl, and get a promise of the first chance in it. If God gives him luck it will be a great rise entirely for him, and plaze goodness I'll give him some help to stock it; but sure we don't know—it's all in the hands of the great God, and we must wait with patience, glory be to His holy name."

Having inspected the oat, potato, and wheat crops, and expressed their hopes and fears on their appearance, Toney repaired to Fehily's farm, which was adjoining, to make the same inspection, and both then went to their respective homes.

During the week Bartle Donohoe, the suitor of Margaret Byrne, came to inform her father of his interview with Earl Fitzwilliam, and his entire success.

It was true that Pat Hanlon was resigning his farm; and the earl wrote a letter to his agent, Captain Johnson, requesting that Bartle Donohoe should have the preference before any one. He was quite delighted with the kind consideration with which the earl inquired after his tenants and their families, making inquiries also after their comforts, hoping the stock had escaped the sickness which was prevalent in a barony not far distant. A widowed tenant of his lordship, who had been deficient in her rent in consequence of the loss of several head of black cattle from this cause, came to ask an extension of time while Bartle was there. The earl expressed great regret at the losses she sustained, assured her she should not only have time, but that, knowing her to be an industrious improving tenant and a widow, she should be allowed for every head of cattle she lost on presenting a statement of their value to the agent. "The captain did not act harshly, did he?" said the earl. "Oh no, indeed, my lord," replied the poor woman, while tears of gratitude filled her eyes,—" oh no, indeed; he only sent for his rent, and sure that's what he had a right to do; but it fretted me not to have it for him, and I made up my mind I'd come and speak to your lordship. I knew I'd be sure to meet with consideration if I'd see you—may God shower his choicest blessings on your house this day! Oh no, my lord, the captain never distressed me a bit." "If he did, I'd distress him," said the earl. "I will not allow such acts to be done on my estate."* Both Bartle and the widow retired blessing God for giving them so good a landlord. Oh, that the landed proprietors of Ireland could only be made to under-

---

* This conversation actually occurred; but since then, unhappily, the papers report him to have become an exterminator like the rest. Such is the force of bad example.

stand their own interests! If they would but make themselves acquainted with the character of the people over whom they exercise so much power, and then act towards them with simple justice, showing that consideration for their feelings which God certainly intended one human being to have for another, what a life of inborn happiness would they not enjoy in this life, not to speak of their prospects in the life to come!

Toney Byrne had now no further opposition to make to his daughter's marriage, and accordingly Margaret and Bartle Donohoe were married in about ten days from his interview with Lord Fitzwilliam. They had a genuine Irish wedding; the table was laid in the long barn, graced with many fine turkeys, geese, chickens, rounds of beef, sirloins of ditto, plum puddings, apple dumplings, every kind of cakes, fruits, etc., and wine and whiskey *ad libitum*. But I presume most of my readers have been to Irish weddings before now, and it is unnecessary to describe how the venerable Father Esmond sat at the head of the table, how Father O'Tool occupied the next seat of distinction, how the parish priest blessed and cut the wedding cake, helping the bridesmaid to the first cut, how she made believe to be eating but reserved the greater part to divide amongst her young friends for the purpose of dreaming on it, how when the priest retired the tables were cleared away, and the fiddlers and pipers and dancers all commenced in earnest, how they danced in the barn and in every room in the house until the small hours of the morning, when the guests, after many affectionate good-byes, took their departure, praying long life and happiness to the young couple. My readers have enjoyed all this before, and I therefore merely glance at it. A few days after the wedding Bartle Donohoe took his bride to his father's, where they were to remain until his own farmhouse was vacated.

The hauling home was another scene of festivity. Her father, eldest brother, and some near relatives, accompanied them. All rode on horseback; Margaret was mounted on a pillion behind her husband. Some miles from Donohoe's farm Bartle's father, his two oldest brothers, and a band of neighbors, came to meet them on horseback and formed a guard of honor to welcome the young bride, who blushingly thanked them for their attention, and smiled through the tears she had been shedding all day after parting with her mother and sister.

"All the world and his wife" were assembled at the farm, and another joyous scene similar to the wedding took place. Next day, after many tears fond embracings, and blessings on his child, Toney Byrne and his escort returned to Glengoulah. They passed Mr. De Courcy's mills on their way home, and met Tom Moody, the under steward, coming out of the office. Calling Toney one side he told him strange news. Mr. De Courcy had received letters from London that morning, announcing the death of Sir Charles Plover. He had been killed in a duel by a colonel in her majesty's life-guards, with whom he had a dispute at play. The melancholy event took place near Dieppe, in France, whither they had gone to evade the law. Sir Charles Plover had never married, consequently the estate must pass into the hands of the nearest of kin, who was his first cousin, the Rev. Samuel Wilson Biggs, who was rector of Christ Church, Nottingham, England.

Poor Toney Byrne heard this news with a sad heart, for though the landlord was nothing to him— none of the tenantry had ever seen him—still he foreboded evil the moment he heard the new landlord was an Anglican minister. "I wonder will Mr. De Courcy act as agent still, Mr. Moody?" asked Toney of the steward. "That's more than any of us can tell, Mr. Byrne; but I don't see any reason why he wouldn't—I'm sure he knows the property better than any one, and he understands the people—

unless he gets tired of it and gives it up himself. I think the new landlord ought to be very glad to give it to him." "God grant he may keep it, then," said Toney, fervently, "for he's a fair and honorable gentleman."

Poor Mrs. Byrne had been inconsolable from the time she parted with her dear child, and renewed her sorrow when she saw her husband returning without her; but she soon dried her eyes when Toney said:

"Don't be foolish, Kitty; give thanks to God that your daughter has a dacent boy and a comfortable home under a good landlord; not at all like her father and mother, I'm afraid. I met Tom Moody at the mills below, and he tells me news came from London this mornin' that Sir Charles is dead, and the new landlord is a Protestant minister; so God between us and harm, this day! But, Kitty, my heart bodes no good to ourselves or our neighbors. I'm afraid there's a black cloud gatherin' a top of Glengoulah hill."

"Oh, Christ protect us! Toney, avic!" exclaimed his wife, arising from her seat with staring eyes. "Is it the truth you're spakin'; or are you only frightenin' me a purpose to keep me from frettin' after Margie?"

"Bedad, it's the truth I'm tellin' you, Kitty; and sorry I am to have to tell it."

"Oh the cross of Christ about us and preserve us!" And Kitty made the holy sign on her forehead, lips, and breast, and courtesied devoutly. "Och, wirrah, wirrah, this day! Luck nor grace can't come where one of them black divils has any hand—God forgive me—but sure I know the breed of old. Don't I mind when my poor brother Andy was put in for beatin' the tithe proctor—God rest his soul, amen!" (Mrs. Bryne certainly meant her brother's soul, not the tithe proctor's). "Didn't my mother go to the minister to ask him to spake a word for the poor boy, seein' he was young and hot in himself, and was aggravated by reason of her bein' offended. Didn't the ould hypocrite snuffle through his nose and tell her she reared her son bad; that she ought to tache him to be meek and humble, and to folly the scriptures, and if he was struck on one cheek to turn the other? My poor mother was the mildest and pacefulest woman that ever lived. You'd wonder if you saw how patient and gentle she looked. To think any one could have the heart to spake that way to her, and she in trouble!—she riz up and walked from the room without another word, she was chokin'."

Young Andy Byrne, who was listening to his mother with flashing eyes and burning cheeks, said quickly: "Mother, who was with my grandmother when he said that?" "No one, alanna; she was loath to take any one with her, afraid they might refuse to let her see the minister if there was another by."

"I wish I was by, and to be as big as I am now; I'd give him a rap in his ould jaw, and I'd see if he'd turn th' other side."

"Oh whist, Andy, avic machree!" said his mother with a shudder; and drawing him towards her she laid his head on her bosom, and passing her hand through his fair clustering hair, she made the sign of the cross on his forehead, murmuring fervently: "God bless my own bouchleen bawn, and mark him to grace, and preserve him from sin, accidents, and dangers."

"Musha, mother!" exclaimed Andy, jumping up and cutting a caper on the floor; "one would think I was goin' to kick the minister now, you're so frightened; 'deed if I was with my grandmother that day I'd give him a polthogue, just to see how he'd take it; he's too ould now if he'd be alive at all, but I suppose the divil got him long ago."

"Oh, fie upon you, Andy, honey! Don't talk that

way; sure you know we're not allowed to judge any one."

"Och musha, mother asthore! Don't I know you and my father and the priest is sayin' that always; but sure I know very well God Almighty has no hand in such ould varmint and hypocrites, and he must belong to one side or the other; anyway it's well for his ould jaw I wasn't near him that day. Hooroosh! there's the spotted calf runnin' through the meadow like mad." And away bounded Andy in high glee for the chase. His mother looked after him with a mixture of pride and sadness. Turning from the door, she said to herself: "Well, hasn't he the noble sperit all out? Thanks and praises be to the great God for all things! He's a Malone to the backbone."

"Tony, who had lit his pipe after entering the house, sat back in the chimney-corner. Keeping his eyes fixed on the fire, and being entirely absorbed in puffing and watching the blaze as it flickered in and out of the turf pile, he heeded not what was passing between his wife and son. Advancing now to meet her, as she turned from watching Andy, he said: "Kitty, I'm after goin' over in my mind the way we're in at present, and I don't like how things look, but I see no way of bettering ourselves; so I come to the conclusion that the best thing we can do is to remember we're in the hands of God, and to go on doin' our duty and lave it all to Him. Thanks be to His holy name we've everything snug and comfortable around us, and we have our rent ready, and what need we care? We never seen Sir Charles's face, and maybe this man would stay in England too, and lave the estate to be managed by Mr. De Courcy, and sure, if he does, it will make no differ to us who is landlord; howsomever, let it go what way it will, we can't better it by frettin' about it, so welcome be the will of God."

Poor Kitty tried hard to take the same philosophic view of affairs as her husband; but it was plain her spirit chafed under the bare idea of holding their farm, which belonged to the Brynes, father and son, for generations, at the will of a member of that body which made itself most obnoxious to the people in all parts of the country, and which poor Kitty had good reason to dread as the bitterest enemy of her faith and race. She therefore merely shook her head, saying with a sigh: "Maybe so, asthore; maybe so; God is good!" and calling Winefred to her they took their snow-white pails and went to the byre to milk the cows, which now came slowly into the yard chewing the cud, and taking observations with their mild intelligent eyes.

CHAPTER IV.

About a month after the wedding of Margaret Byrne her mother and sister were busy spinning away to make a stock of house linen for the winter, Mrs. Byrne having sent a chest full to Margaret as her mother's wedding gift; and her stock being greatly reduced thereby, they were working away to replace it, when a horse and rider turned into the front yard, and stopping at the porch the rider alighted. He was a stout portly man, apparently about fifty years of age, with a mild benevolent countenance, his hair slightly sprinkled with silver, and his whole air, garb and bearing carrying unmistakable evidence of the true gentleman. Mrs. Byrne, hurriedly calling Mike to hold the horse, ran out, and, courtesying, welcomed Mr. De Courcy to the farm. Taking off his hat he entered the farm-house, saluted Winefred kindly, and, taking a seat, complimented her on her industry, inquired what she had been spinning (for Winnie arose to make obeisance on his entrance, but did not through politeness resume her noisy occupation), and whether she found it productive; asked Mrs. Byrne after her husband and the boys, and what progress they were making; inquired how the young summer stock got on, and whether she still bore off the palm for her butter, poultry, etc. Mrs. Byrne gave him all the satisfaction she could. He admired the neat arrangements of the flower beds in the grass plot before the door, and seemed highly pleased with the look of comfort and industry which the whole place presented, not forgetting to note the flitches of bacon and coils of hogs' puddings suspended from the ceiling. He then told Mrs. Byrne they were going to have a resident landlord.

Unlike Sir Charles Plover, who had never been in Ireland since he was a boy, the Rev. Mr. Biggs was coming to reside amongst them. Orders had been received to put Glengoulah Castle in immediate repair, and artizans of all kinds were coming to decorate it in the highest style of art. Splendid furniture was ordered from Paris, and a regular suite of English servants coming to take charge of all domestic arrangements. Mr. Biggs expected to be settled in his future residence by Christmas.

"I understand," said Mr. De Courcy, "he has effected an exchange with the present rector of this parish, and intends to rule in the double capacity of landlord and rector."

"Well, the Lord break hard fortune before us! But I'm mighty sorry to hear it, your honor; I'm afraid luck and grace and happiness are leavin' us behind them;" and poor Mrs. Byrne rocked to and fro, as was her wont when her mind was troubled. "Oh, don't say that, Mrs. Byrne," said the agent, cheerfully. "Don't you know one of the worst evils of Ireland is absenteeism, or the landlord making his residence in a foreign land and not looking personally after the condition of his tenantry? And now Mr. Biggs is going to repair that evil by residing amongst you all, and watching over your interests."

"Oh no, sir; it may be true what you say, that a landlord has a right to look to his tenants. If they all done it, then one would be ashamed of the other not to act like a gentleman; but where there's only one they're more like to be a tyrant. Anyway, may God long preserve your honor! We didn't know the bad of an absentee landlord while we had you. Oh, Mr. De Courcy, dear! sure you won't lave us?"

"I really cannot tell yet, Mrs. Byrne. I should be very sorry, indeed, to part with the tenantry of Glengoulah estate, for I have found them thoroughly upright, peaceable people, kind neighbors, and good friends. I really feel a kind of affection for every one on the estate, and I believe they love me too." Mr. De Courcy's voice trembled as he said the latter words. It was evident (though he did not express it) he boded no good from the clerical landlord. As for poor Mrs. Byrne, she and Winnie cried outright, and could not speak a word. "However, it is all foolish to think on it yet," said Mr. De Courcy, brightening up. "We may be pleased all round by the change. The English landlords are very kind and just to their tenantry in their own country, and Mr. Biggs may be one of the best of them for aught we know. Remember, I know as little about him as any of you. Rest assured, Mrs. Byrne, I shall not give up the management of the estate as long as I can retain it with honor to myself and good to the tenantry. Please tell Byrne to bring his lease to my office during the course of the week, as I am putting my affairs in order." And so taking a smiling adieu, he patted Mike on the head, slipped a half-crown into his hand unknown to his mother, and mounting his horse rode away.

Mr. De Courcy, after leaving Toney Byrne's farm, rode on about three miles over the beautiful "Cascade mountain," as it was poetically and truthfully named, for hundreds of tiny waterfalls came bound ing through the variegated shrubs, over moss-covered rocks, and made the hills musical with their murmuring glee as they rushed down to meet the Avon and flow into the lovely vale of Ovoca. Beyond this hill, and between it and another cone-shaped hill, crowned on top with a clump of mountain ash, was a verdant plain about a quarter of a mile wide. In the centre of this plain nestled a large thriving village, almost pretending to be a town (in America it would be called a city). Here was a green where an annual cattle-fair was held, and at the end of this green stood a goodly-sized stone building of cruciform shape, destitute of ornament save a stone cross of modest dimensions at the termination of the gable, which faced the entrance. Over the principal door, which was a double one grained in oak, were the initials I. H. S., so well known to every Catholic to signify "Jesus, Saviour of men." The back of this building was shaded by a grove of oak, elm, and ash-trees, commingled. Beside it stood a magnificent elm towering above all, and bearing high up in its branches a bell of humble size, from which a simple rope most unpoetically dangled, or was tied around the trunk; nevertheless that modest bell made music amongst the mountain echoes, as from its leafy spire it called the faithful children of the

Church to come and assist at the adorable sacrifice. The ground on which this building stood covered a considerable space, and was enclosed by a rustic paling, which could now be scarcely discerned through the thickly-interlaced hedge of sweet-brier and wild roses. Within this enclosure, and all around the building, with the exception of the neatly-gravelled pathway, the grass was thick, soft as Genoa velvet, and literally bespangled with daisies and buttercups. Long green mounds were strewn around: some with head-stones, simple and quaint enough; some with a plain stone cross; some with a rose-bush at the head; but the greater number with no mark save that known to the eye of affection, which never makes a mistake. All told "the short and simple annals of the poor." Dear reader, this is the village and parish chapel of Tinmanogue, and the little churchyard is the principal burying-place of the neighboring hills. That substantial-looking cottage beside the chapel, embowered amongst the trees, with its bright flower-garden in front, is the residence of the beloved parish priest of Tinmanogue and his almost equally beloved curate. The hillsides and the plains around are dotted with farm-houses and the cottages of the farm laborers, all bearing the same look of neatness and comfort, for it is still the estate of the late Sir Charles Plover, and now the property of the Rev. Samuel Wilson Biggs.

Mr. De Courcy on coming in sight of Tinmanogue let the bridle fall loosely on the neck of his horse, and turning to look on every side, surveyed the lovely prospect with feelings of pleasure and regret. He felt that inward satisfaction which every just man feels in looking upon the effects of his good works, and then came the sense of deep regret which he could not shake off, for he knew he would soon be as a stranger amongst those farms whose prosperity he had watched with paternal care; and though he well knew he would ever live in the warm affections of the grateful people, he also knew they would soon be surrounded by trials from which he could not extricate them.

Arriving at the shady cottage he was shown into the modest parlor. The furniture was plain, substantial, and beautifully clean. It bore a strong resemblance in many points to Goldsmith's celebrated room, for the sanded floor was there, and the clock ticking behind the door; the green boughs were in the fire-place, and the chest of drawers contriving to pay a double debt—not in the same sense, however, for it was not a bed either by night or by day; but the top part was a writing desk and bureau, being the depository of the parish registries, and all other important papers, while the under part was a chest of drawers; it was of old fashioned mahogany, and had massive handles and ornamental key-holes of the brightest brass. In place of "the twelve good rules and royal game of goose," the walls were hung with a plain, neat paper, and suspended thereon were some rare pictures—for Father Esmond was a lover of the beautiful in art, and brought those with him from France. Ireland in his young days had no means of educating her sons for the priesthood, as the odious penal laws were still in force. Father Esmond, therefore, had been sent, with many other students, to France, to study his ecclesiastical course, and had returned a learned and holy priest.

Between the windows was an exquisite engraving of the "Ecce Homo." Over the bureau a well-executed copy of Carlo Dolci's "Holy Family." Over the sideboard a fine engraving of Raphael's "Last Supper." In the recesses of the fire-place were the "Annunciation" and the "Baptism of Our Lord," both matches, finely finished, and in old-fashioned oval frames. But the masterpiece of all, and the glory of the old pastor's heart, was an old oil painting over the mantelpiece—it was the "Repentance of St. Peter," and was indeed a gem.

Mr. De Courcy, who was an enthusiastic admirer of the fine arts, stood entranced before it for some time, and then passed to the others. Looking through a side window he saw an equally fine living picture. A venerable man, evidently more than eighty summers, with a benign and smiling countenance, was standing beside a clear pond in the hollow of a verdant field. He was a little above the middle height and of a rotund form, his dress was black save a pair of dark-gray stockings which encased his stout, well-formed legs, which, whenever he went abroad, or expected company, were again covered by black-cloth leggings, terminating in a pair of thick shoes fastened by silver buckles of a departed age. On his head he wore the three-cornered tonsure cap peculiar to his sacred office; his long snow-white hair flowing underneath was stirred by the gentle breeze. In his hand he held a small basket from which he scattered wheat and breadcrumbs to a numerous flock of geese, ducks, and chickens, alternately scolding, petting, and laughing heartily at the scramble amongst the fowls. A couple of aristocratic ducks, disdaining to enter the crowd of beggars, stood a little apart with an eye cocked up, as much as to say, "Here we are, waiting in dignified expectation." They were now addressed: "Indeed, then, you shall, Juno, have some nice crumbs, yourself and Ceres, just because you are not fighting about it. Down, Cæsar; down, sir;" and away went ducks and geese plunging into the pond, while the chickens with extended wings ran screaming away to the barn-yard. This commotion amongst them was excited by Mrs. Malone opening the little yard-gate leading to the field to tell his reverence how a visitor awaited him, contrary, however, to the express injunctions of Mr. De Courcy, who assured the house-keeper he was in no hurry, and would prefer awaiting the leisure of Father Esmond.

Mrs. Malone, after delaying a little, got on the fidgets, and the moment she opened the gate out bounded Cæsar, a splendid mastiff, who had been wistfully watching the gate ever since his master's egress, and now sent the poor chickens flying in all directions. Father Esmond entered the house immediately. "My dear friend, Mr. De Courcy," said he, extending both hands; "I am quite rejoiced to see you; you are heartily welcome to Tinmanogue; bless my soul how glad I am to see you! And you are here some time, Mrs. Malone tells me, and would not let me be called—now what's that for? You wanted to surprise me, did you?" His eye now caught a stray glance of Mr. De Courcy's wandering over the fire-place.

'Ah, ha! I see it all now; I have the secret. You were examining my 'St. Peter'." Mr. De Courcy pleaded guilty. "Well, I forgive you—it is not every day you meet with a picture like that. My dear sir, that picture would take whole weeks to view properly. Many an hour I remain before it and yet discover new beauties continually. Now just stand in this light and catch the expression of that face. Look! there is true repentance for you!"

"Indeed, Father Esmond, I never saw anything more perfect; he seems truly the rugged fisherman. I fancy he has just moored his smack, awaiting the morrow's dawn to be off again."

"Yes, just so; the weather-beaten fisherman—his hair seems to stand out as if still blown about by the gales from lake Galilee; his garment flies open and bares his breast to the breeze, but he heeds not all that. Oh, my friend! just look at those sun-embrowned hands clasped together so closely; don't you think they seem to quiver with the anguish of that soul upon which Jesus has cast a pitying yet reproachful glance? Don't those ears still seem to ring with the crowing of that cock which first warned him of his terrific sin? those lips seem trying to utter words of heartfelt sorrow, but cannot for the choking sobs? Then look at those tears streaming down the furrowed cheeks; those eyes incessantly filling, raised to heaven with an expression of intensest love for his Divine Master, and agonizing contrition for having denied Him. Oh, Peter! Peter! how many of us follow you in your fall; how few in your repentance!"

Mr. De Courcy, who seemed spellbound by the eloquence of his host, now turned to look at him. His cap was in his hand, his white hair flowing back, and his aged eyes filled with tears: he looked almost as fine a picture as the blessed Peter himself. A new emotion filled the heart of Mr. De Courcy; he could not account for it, but he seemed to feel himself quite insignificant, and would fain have remained silent and unobserved. Soon Father Esmond, wiping his eyes, cried out: "Bless my soul! that picture makes me forget everything. Sit down, my dear sir, sit down; you will pardon the forgetfulness of an old man. I hope Mrs. De Courcy and the little people are well. How are matters progressing at Glengoulah? I suppose the old castle is putting on its grand look, as of old."

"Yes, indeed; the castle and the demesne of Glengoulah are fit for any nobleman to reside in. I wish they were about to be occupied by some one worthy of such a princely inheritance. Indeed,

Father Esmond, I came to visit you to-day for the purpose of having a conversation with you on this very subject. I am anxious to know if you have any idea who this Biggs is; have you heard anything of him?"

"I have not the slightest suspicion who he is; nor, indeed, do I much care. As long as you are the agent we don't care who the landlord is, and for this reason I never made an inquiry on the subject; but there's the old man's selfishness breaking out again! I'm forgetting how very unpleasant it would be for you if he should happen to be a disagreeable man. I wish he had stayed where he was born."

"Well, Father Esmond, I had a suspicion from the first that he was the person of whom I heard my cousin William speak when he came home from Oxford. I thought the name was the same, but not feeling certain I wrote my cousin on the subject, related what I had heard of the character of our new landlord, and begged he would describe, as accurately as possible, his old class-mate at Oxford. He had started for Germany before my letter reached his home, but they forwarded it to him, and he replied from Dresden. It only reached me yesterday."

Pulling out a pocket-book, Mr. De Courcy took a letter from it which he handed to Father Esmond. While the priest was occupied reading the letter his guest again stood before the "St. Peter;" and as he went afresh over every lineament the words of the venerable Father seemed to burn into his soul. Father Esmond, having read the letter twice over with the greatest care, folded it and returned it with a sigh. "God help my poor people if the person your cousin speaks of be the same Biggs; and I fear it is, for the points of resemblance are very strong. I fear there are sad times in store for the tenantry. Oh, Mr. De Courcy, my dear friend, let me implore you not to abandon my poor people. You are their only earthly salvation. Should you resign he would easily find a creature of his own to appoint who would be ready for any mean employment."

"God forgive me! I'd rather have the wickedest old sinner than one of those canting, psalm-singing crew. The sinner might be converted; but those creatures are so full of self-glorification that they have no room for the glory of God, and if they don't begin they certainly end with hypocrisy."

"You may rest assured, Father Esmond, it will be the last resort left to honor when I resign the Glengoulah estate. I need hardly tell you that it is not for its pecuniary profits I will hold it under such a man. I don't need it, happily; but my affections have become bound up with the tenantry. I am not a very demonstrative character, and I'm sure many of the poor fellows have thought me exacting, but I love them as though they were my own children. I have ever found them punctual and upright in all their dealings with me, and ready to adopt any suggestion I made for the improvement of their farms; indeed, I think they took an especial pride in following my advice, just to show their confidence in me; for some of them, I know, could not see the drift of my arrangements in the beginning, though they saw the benefit of them afterwards. It will be one of the most painful epochs of my life if I am ever compelled to resign the management of this estate, and I hope fervently I may be spared it."

Poor Father Esmond was quite overcome by these observations, and, making a great effort to control his feelings, he said : "My dear friend, there is not a man, woman, or child in Glengoulah but would die for you. You must not leave us. God is stronger than the enemy; we will all importune Heaven, and ———"

"Oh, Father Esmond, no ; please do not let the tenantry know I heard anything of the landlord — it would be extremely imprudent. In the first place, we have only a suspicion—a very strong one, it is true, but still a mere suspicion—that he and this Oxford man are the same person; and then, if the people through my means become prejudiced against him it would be sure to reach his ears, and we might look out for separation truly; and, moreover, we would deserve it too. No, no; I brought this letter to put you on your guard, as you might see some way of foiling him if he should contemplate a crusade against the religion of the people. This is in strict confidence."

"Pardon me, my dear Mr. De Courcy; I was quite taken off my guard by the bare idea of losing you. Of course you are perfectly right; I see the impropriety of letting any one know. You may rest easy: the contents of that letter shall never pass my lips until you release me yourself from silence."

"Enough, Father; I must go now. It is getting late."

"Upon my word, you sha'n't leave me until you take pot luck with me; my dinner will be ready an hour from this, and Father O'Tool will be home and will amuse you with his droll stories. He's the life and soul of Tinmanogue."

"I am very much obliged, Father Esmond; but it is quite impossible I could accept of your kind invitation to-day. There are two gentlemen to dine with me—tourists; who came to see the vale of Ovoca. I met them this morning accidentally, and they promised to be at my house at six o'clock."

"Well! well! I am very sorry for my sake; but the duties of hospitality can't be postponed, so I give you up for this day—but you mustn't take the curse of the house with you.

"Mrs. Malone, will you be kind enough to bring the decanters here; and where's that cake I heard you boasting about? I think you said it went very nicely with raspberry jam! We'll put it to the test ma'am, if you please."

Mrs. Malone, who had been expecting some such summons, came in arrayed in a black-satin gown which had seen better days, and a cap decorated with blue gauze ribbons. She bore a tray, with a goodly array of wine-glasses, decanters, cake, and preserves, with her best china plates, and came near demolishing a glass in her efforts to place the tray on the table and make a most gracious courtesy at the same time for Mr. De Courcy's especial benefit. With the kindness of a true gentleman he saluted the good woman, told her he had heard of her high reputation in the manufacture of cakes and preserves, and was resolved to show how much he appreciated such useful acquirements. Mrs. Malone assured his honor it was only his kindness to say so, not but she *could* make cakes if she only had the least idea that they would be tasted by so capable a judge, but that one now on the tray was only a poor specimen of her art, etc., etc. It was easy to see, however, that she was mightily pleased, and making two more dignified courtesies—one at the table, and one at the door—she made her exit, ever afterwards declaring that "Mr. De Courcy was the nicest and most knowledgeable gentleman that ever came to Tinmanogue."

To say truth, the refreshments were all the best; and the agent, having partaken of them, requested Father Esmond to try and get over to his house soon. Mrs. De Courcy would be quite delighted to see him, and he wanted to show him some new machinery he had got in the mill.

"Ah, my dear friend! it is little visiting I can do now. I suffer much at times from asthma, but praises be to God! I have had a long life of good health, and must expect some shadow of the coming event which can't be far distant now."

"Oh, you mustn't say that, Father; I trust it is many, many years distant."

"Well! well! God's holy will be done as He

pleases, my son. I would like very much indeed to go and see your family; if possible I will do so."

Mr. De Courcy leaned over and in an undertone whispered, "Meantime, Father, please remember me in your petitions to Heaven, and when you are viewing your St. Peter."

"Indeed, then, I will, my dear friend and child. God bless you!"

Mr. De Courcy vaulted into his saddle, and, raising his hat once more to the venerable figure standing on the door-step, galloped up the hill and was out of sight in a minute.

CHAPTER V.

THE long-expected time came at length when there arrived at Glengoulah Castle troops of servants and piles of luggage from England; and, about a week afterwards, the Rev. Samuel Wilson Biggs, his lady the Rev. Mrs. Samuel Biggs, his two maiden sisters the Misses Biggs, a valet, and two waiting maids, drove up in two carriages and four to the grand sweep before the castle hall; whereupon there was great commotion amongst the hired retainers, and a great clattering of dishes in the culinary apartments, accompanied by an odor bearing sure evidence that the comforts of the inward man were being attended to.

A few days after the arrival of the family the two waiting women took counsel together, during breakfast hour, in the dressing-room of the Rev. mistress.

"La me!" said Miss Jemima Jenkins (the Rev. mistress's own maid) to Miss Amelia Hopkins, who had the felicity to wait on the spinster sisters of their Rev. master—"La me! I verily believe we shall mope to death in this hold castle, perched hon the top of the 'ill; just look out of this winder, and see what a frightful 'ight we are." And the two young ladies gazed into the valley below, just at the point "where the bright waters meet." Then they cast their eyes on the opposite hills, covered with verdure, though it was the first week of December, and on the thousand waterfalls and silver streams—one of the most picturesquely beautiful scenes the eye of man could wish to repose on in this world. Drawing in her head, Miss Jemima Jenkins exclaimed, with a sigh: "I shall ask mistress to raise my wages. It is evident there is no chance of society in such a wild place! I should die, I know I should, in one quarter."

"Yes," rejoined Miss Amelia Hopkins; "and only think! the coachman, footman, and two grooms are all married men; it is perfectly unbearable! I too shall demand 'igher wages, or I sha'n't wait on Miss Biggs, nor Miss Rachel neither, so I sha'n't."

"And I heard mistress tell master this morning," said Miss Jemima Jenkins, " that she didn't see how she was ever a goin' to live among such barbarous people. But la! master is *so* religious! he told her she must look upon it as a trial sent her by the Lord, and try to bear it with Christian fortitude. He said:

Mistress, and Miss Biggs, and Miss Rachel, and you, and me, and all the servants, should try and reform the people on the estate. 'I am sure, sir,' says I, 'if I had come hair to such a rich hestate I should prefer to pay hagents to manage it for me, and live in a civilized country myself;' but I do believe if there's a saint on hearth master's one. He turned up the wites of his heyes, and says he, in a solemn voice, 'What you say, my dear Jenkins, would be quite acceptable to a worldly-minded man, but my bowels yearn with compassion for those creatures who are half savages by nature, and whose steps run after iniquity; it will be my care to regenerate them in a new baptism, so to speak, and bring their feet into the path of the Lord.' Oh, 'Opkins, you never 'eard such sighs as he drew up from the very bottom of his stomach; it gave me the 'art burn to 'ear 'em."

"Well! I don't care if he is so religious, I *haint*—and so I just intend to do as little work as ever I can; and I'm a goin' to see if I can't make some himpression on the 'art of Mr. Jones, the 'ed butler. I've singled him out as my game, so see you don't look at him!" shaking her finger playfully at her companion. "La me!" cried Miss Jemima, with a contemptuous toss of her head, which made all the pink ribbons in her fancy cap flutter for five seconds,

"I think mistress's own maid may look 'igher. I haint got such low tastes, I can assure you, 'Opkins; and if I do amuse myself a talkin' to Mr. Thompson, master's valet, it is only till I can find society capable of appreciating me."

"Well done, my lady Pimlico," cried Miss Amelia, mimicking the voice of her friend Jenkins,— "Well, I never! So we're puttin' on hairs, are we? He, he, he. My heyes! wont I have fun in the servants' 'all to-night. I suppose we'll begin to get religion too, like master, and turn up the wites of our heyes and sing psalms"— and the tantalizing young lady began to sing in a nasal tone:

"Oh! there's a 'appy land, far, far away."

Suddenly the bell of Miss Biggs's dressing-room rang furiously, and at the same moment the sickly step of the Rev. mistress was heard ascending the stairs, which caused the instantaneous cessation of the hymn, and the sudden transition of Miss Amelia Hopkins from the front to the rear of the castle, while the offended person of Miss Jemima Jenkins quickly passed from an easy, dignified position in an arm-chair before the looking-glass, to one of most bustling activity, with something in her fair hand which bore a suspicious resemblance to a dusting-brush. For the present we shall leave the afflicted inmates of Glengoulah Castle to the terrible calamities consequent upon a residence amongst a barbarous people, and see what the savage tenantry are about.

Toney Byrne took his lease to Mr. De Courcy's office, at the mills, as directed, and was told to leave it there, for the Rev. landlord had not yet attended to any business; but Mr. De Courcy would be sure to call his earliest attention to it, and to some others which also required renewal.

Some weeks had elapsed, Christmas had come and gone, the new year had dawned, but Toney received no summons to visit the office in order to sign his new lease. At length, in the second week of January, at the oft-repeated request of his wife, Toney went to the office once more. He was received as kindly as ever by Mr. De Courcy, who told him he regretted very much that his lease was still unsigned by the landlord. "I have urged him frequently, Byrne, and he kept putting me off upon one pretext or another until last week, when he positively refused to sign any lease until he made himself acquainted with the character and condition of the tenantry. However, it wont be long now until the March gales come, and perhaps he may give orders to have the leases ready by rent day. Meantime

I am quite willing to have the character of each tenant and the condition of each holding scrutinized, for I am proud of the whole."

"Yes, sir, thanks be to God, your honor needn't be afraid or ashamed of any of us."

"Mr. Biggs is going to have a new church built on the demesne, and a school-house, he tells me, so that will give a good deal of employment."

"Ah, what in the world does he want with another church, sir? Sure the parish church of Tinmanogue has only a congregation of seven persons, and where will he find scholars for his schools?"

"Why, you forget, Byrne, that his own establishment at the castle would make a numerous congregation; and, as they are all English, I presume they are Protestants likewise. Perhaps, too, many of them are married, and have young families; and if so, the ladies will require some useful occupation, and so may turn teachers. And, perhaps"—Mr. De Courcy smiled quietly—"some of the tenantry may be glad to avail themselves of so good an opportunity to educate their children, and send them to this school too."

"Oh no, bedad, sir! Sorra a fear of that. If the good gentleman is goin' to build churches, or schools aither, for the benefit of the Glengoulah people, he had better keep his money. A good mornin' Mr. De Courcy!"

"Good morning, Byrne."

As Toney was approaching his home he met Tom Moody, whom he invited in to "take the weight off his limbs, and have a draw of the pipe." He told Mrs. Byrne "a power of news" about the Biggs family, and their doings at the castle. Indeed, Kitty had been dying to see the same Tom, and had come out upon the road a dozen times when she espied a hat like his coming down the road. With a long stocking tucked under her arm, at the toe of which she was busy with her needles, Mrs. Byrne would come out and look down the road in the opposite direction from where the owner of the hat was coming, as if expecting somebody. After gazing a while she would turn round carelessly, intending, if it should be Tom, to say, "Why, then, now, is that yourself, Tom Moody? Who'd ever think to see you here the mornin'? Come in and rest a while." And so she would be sure to hear all the news, for Tom was an incorrigible gossip, and had a knack of worming himself in with strangers, and by finding out a little here, and a little there, and "putting that and that together," as he said himself, it was quite wonderful what shrewd guesses he made.

Poor Mrs. Byrne, however, had come out so often, and looked down the road so intently, and turned round so innocently (expecting to accost Tom) every time encountering the eyes of a stranger, that she almost despaired of ever seeing Tom Moody again. She had kept her own counsel, however, and never mentioned her movements to any one, for she knew how much Toney discountenanced gossiping. As Tom now made his appearance with her husband she accosted him kindly, but with the most diplomatic *nonchalance*, inquired after all the neighbors in his parts (Tom was a bachelor), and glancing carelessly at his hat, which he held between his knees, she requested to be allowed to put it on the table. As she laid it down she took a second look at it, and said, " Why, then, Tom Moody, did you pass down this road three or four times this week ?"

" No, indeed, ma'am ; if I did you may be sure I'd step in to bid you the time of day."

" 'Deed, that's what made me wonder ; and yet I certainly seen a hat like this one goin' down the road, whoever wore it."

" You did, Mrs. Byrne ? are you sure of that, ma'am ?"

" 'Deed, I never was surer of anything ; when I seen your hat now it brought it to my mind."

"Ahem! I see now how the cat jumps; what kind of a lookin' man was he, Mrs. Byrne?"

Kitty, unwilling to confess she was outside of her own premises, said, evasively, "I just seen the hat over the hedge, and not bein' a common one it took my eye."

"Well, ma'am, that must be no other man but Sandy McGlauren, the Scotch steward; he has a hat for all the world the comrade of mine; but he's a gradle taller nor I am, and has great big bones. Well, ma'am, if there's a head goin', divil alive it's the same Sandy; he's as deep as a draw-well. And so he was up through the farms! Bedad, I don't like the look of that, Mr. Byrne," turning to Toney. "I don't like to see such cattle rovin' through the hills, so I don't. I wouldn't say now but he was calculatin' the value of every farm, and that a rise in the rent would be soon recommended."

"Tut, tut, man!" exclaimed Toney, who was always disposed to see the bright and peaceful side of everything—"Tut, tut! Don't you know he's a stranger, and it's only natural he'd like to see the country he has come to live in, and to examine the quality of the land too, and see if it's like his own? I don't see anything in that but what we'd do ourselves, if we were in his place."

"Well, wait till you see, Mr. Byrne. I just can tell what them lads is thinkin' of. There's not a wink on me!" at the same time winking very hard with both eyes, to show his great cleverness.

"'Deed, honest man, it's you I belave," chimed in the good woman; "but sure this man of mine won't give ear to anything he hears. I do be as mad as a March hare with him sometimes. The childer can put their finger in his eye and he can't see it."

"Well, now, Kitty, where's the use of judging any one till you know they're guilty—it isn't fair— and we wouldn't like it to be done to ourselves. I like to judge every one fair and square until I find them goin' wrong."

"Why, then, indade, Mr. Byrne, it's little you'll see that's fair or square from the same Sandy, or his master aither, if I'm a livin' man; but time 'ill tell —God keep us all from harm."

"Oh! amen, Tom, honey!" said poor Mrs. Byrne, fervently; and then she began to question him on all he knew of the Biggs family.

"And what kind of a lookin' man is the minister?"

"A mighty mane lookin' little man, Mrs. Byrne, as ever you seen. How old is your Andy now?"

"He's just risin' fourteen."

"Well, the sorra taste bigger nor Andy he is—God bless the boy; but he's most as black as your shoe—no, not so black as that; but I'll tell you now for all the world what he looks like, and sorra word of lie I'm tellin'—he looks like a chimley sweep that was after givin' his face a kind of wash, what we call 'a lick and a promise,'—now that's the very color of his skin; and he has the schaminist eye you ever looked at, and wid all a mighty down mane look."

"Oh, then the curse of the crows on him! Where was he comin' at all at all among dacent people? Did you ever see the mistress at all?"

"See her? 'Deed, I'll engage I did; and more than onst, too."

"Is *she* pretty itself?"

"Pretty? Musha, Mrs. Byrne, where would such a speciment of a man get a pretty woman—eh, now?"

"Why the dickens go from her, sure? We heard she was a lord's daughter."

"So she is, ma'am; a speretual lord's; that is, a Protestant Bishop."

"Oh, persume to her!" said Mrs. Byrne, contemptuously; "if that be all, sure of course we couldn't expect much dacency from her. *She's* black lookin' too, I'll be bound?"

"No; but she's the livin' picture of a yalla mullott (mulatto); I mane in the color of her skin. I seen a yalla mullott last summer when I was up in Dublin—I went on an errand from the master to the counsellor. Well, there was an American ship lyin' in the docks, and I should go on boord of her wid the rest of the crowd to be sure, and there I seen the mullott. She was the steward's wife, I belave, and attended the ladies' cabin. Her skin looked like a bar of yalla soap that had the measles, but for all she was a fine soncy lookin' woman, and had the darlintist pair of eyes you could wish to see. Well, the minister's lady has such another skin; but, be my sowkins, she can't hould a candle to the mullott in any other respect."

"Is she a big woman?"

"Her height is fair enough, but the divil such a quare made woman ever I seen; she's the very figure of a broomstick, and hasn't a bit on her bones. She has quare dead-lookin' hair, and not as much of it on her whole head as Miss Winny there—God bless the colleen—has in one of them locks that hangs over her laughin' eye. Her nose, chin and elbows is like raziers; and as for her jaw bone, it's so sharp that I'm sure if Samson had it he'd kill more Philistines wid it than he kilt wid the jaw bone of the ass that's wrote about in the Scriptures."

"Well, bad cess to you! out of my sight, Tom Moody, that I mightn't sin, but my heart's broke laughin' at you; but you're the fine lad, so you are."

"Upon my sowl I'm not tellin' you a word of lie, ma'am. Wait till you see her; they say she's half the time dyin', and must have all kinds of attention from mornin' till night. She has a great high-flyer of a watin' maid leapin' round her all the time wid smellin'-bottles and head-dresses. His two sisters is the very mott of himself—small, black, and mane lookin'—but they're all dressed so grand, my dear, and has such airs about them, and spake so fine you'd take them to be rale quality if you didn't know who they wor." For all she laughed so heartily at Tom's description of the minister's family, poor Mrs. Byrne felt her heart sink at the prospect of having the future destiny of the Byrnes entrusted to such keeping. Day or night she could not rest, her duties became irksome, and she would sit for hours brooding over coming shadows, although her fingers were busy at the knitting. Soon she became fretful and impatient, and would fly off to Mrs. Fehily or some other neighbor to hold converse and try to dive into the future intentions of the landlord.

But day after day passed, and Mrs. Byrne grew more restless. At length she thought of a plan—it was to visit Father Esmond at Tinmanogue, and have his reverence's opinion on the state of the case. Having once conceived the project she gave Toney no peace until he consented to go.

"Now's the time, Toney, before the spring work comes on, for we'll be all too busy then, and can't spare any of the bastes. Father Esmond is a long-headed man and has great exparience—and more be token he's a livin' saint and his advice is good. And it will aise our minds if it won't do anything else, so let us saddle Puss in the name of God, and put on the pillion and be off in the mornin' early, and then we'll have plenty of time to see his reverence, and be home early after with the help of God."

"Well, Kitty, I'm very loath to trouble his reverence with our affairs, since he has the whole business of the parish to attend to; but indade I'll overcome my dislike if it 'll only aise your mind, for I never seen you so unaisy about anything. You're like a hen on a hot griddle, so you are; and indade it's glad I am you thought of somethin' to give you relief; so let us be off as you say to-morrow mornin' in God's name."

CHAPTER VI.

"Two travellers might be seen wending their way" down the Cascade hill one cold morning at the beginning of February. The wind swept moaning through the ravines, and made a hollow murmuring through the leafless branches; and between each gust a heavy drizzling rain was trying to fall, but was caught up by a stiff nor'easter before it reached the earth, and blown about in every direction.

The travellers, one of whom was a woman, were on horseback—the woman seated on a pillion behind her husband—both well clad, and with shawls tied over their hats. The horse, a sober philosophical sort of animal, jogged on perfectly unmindful of wind or rain. He held the bit in his mouth, and, with hanging lip, and eyes fixed on the road before him, seemed to look with scornful defiance on the little gusts which jumped out at every winding of the road from behind rocks and stumps of trees, and battering his ears and nose, sent his mane flying into an erect position, then retired to their hiding-places, and running along the hillsides were ready for him again at the next turning. Our four-footed friend, however, had evidently made up his mind not to be daunted by such insignificant obstacles as the weather could present, being perfectly conversant with all its powers; and he accordingly jogged on in the same sing-song trot which he had commenced on leaving home in the morning, and never varied his pace until pulled up by his rider at the residence of the parish priest of Tinmanogue.

The cottage was no longer hidden amongst the trees; for the foliage had departed, and the bare vines hung dangling from the housetop, sometimes rapping on the panes as the wind blew them hither and thither, like vines in distressed circumstances which were begging for admission from the winter's storm. The scene, however, was not so much changed as one would suppose from the season; the evergreens in front of the house still proudly bore their green banners, the mountain ash hung out myriads of scarlet berries, and the ever-verdant grass looked soft as velvet still, though the mountain breezes chased the lights and shadows in quick succession over its surface. The only effect winter could produce was to cause the daisies and buttercups to hide their heads in slumber, awaiting the breath of spring to reanimate them.

Toney Byrne, alighting from his horse, assisted his wife to dismount. Fastening the bridle to one of the trees by the roadside, they entered the priest's garden, knocked at the hall-door, and, upon inquiring for Father Esmond, were shown into the back parlor, which he seldom left now, as it was a warm room, and he was much afflicted with asthma. The venerable gentleman sat at a round table near the fire-place, attired as we last saw him, with the addition of a cloak thrown over his shoulders. The old pleasant smile was there, indicating kindness and hospitality. His table was full of books and writing materials, and in the centre of it stood a neatly-carved ivory crucifix on a pedestal of ebony, and at its foot lay his well-worn breviary. He arose on Toney's entrance, welcomed him and his wife to Tinmanogue, and having shaken them warmly by the hands, made them sit down in the ample chimney, where an immense turf-fire was blazing. Having ascertained the mode by which they travelled, he sent his boy to put the horse in the stable and feed him.

After inquiring for their family and the neighbors round, the priest asked after Margaret and her young husband, prophesying the future prosperity of so worthy and virtuous a couple. The father and mother were proud of the encomiums passed on "their little girl," and thanked his reverence gratefully.

"But oh, Father Esmond, asthore!" said Mrs. Byrne, "the heart within me is sore at the way things is goin' to be, I'm afeared, sir; and that's what brought us to see your reverence to-day. I told Toney I could not rest till I seen you and got some consolation, so we made it up that we'd ride over the hills in spite of the heavy mist and the drivin' wind; for indade, Father honey, the wind is drivin' no faster than the black thoughts is runnin' through my mind."

"Well, to spake the truth, your reverence, I don't like how things looks myself; but still and all, I think Kitty takes things too much to heart, and I'd be glad if your reverence would give her a good scoldin'; she'll sicken herself, so she will, if she goes on at this rate."

"My dear friends, have patience. Don't you know God never abandons those who put their trust in Him? What is troubling your minds? Tell me how you are situated regarding your lease?"

"Well, sir, you see the Byrnes, father and son, for years upon years held a lease for the life of the landlord, and there was a special request put in the body of it that the next landlord would continue the same, by raisin of their bein' of the old stock, and havin' given paceable possession in generations gone of Glengoulah Castle and lands to the ancestors of the Plover family. But now, your reverence, this man is not a direct heir, but is come of a mighty low English breed, I hear; and as we're entirely at his mercy, sure it's no wonder we'd be unaisy, though I do be tryin' to persuade Kitty that the day often clears up and the sun shines out when the mornin' looks dark."

"Well, Toney, I don't see as yet that you have any cause to fear; it is surely not possible that Mr. Biggs would eject one of the best tenants on his estate without cause, and he has no fault nor cannot have any with you, I am sure. I know myself, from conversations I had with Mr. De Courcy, that he has a very high regard for you, and he would not be a party to any injustice; he knows the Byrnes made that farm what it is, from being wild mountain land and bog, by the hard labor of their hands and the sweat of their brows. Oh, no! my dear children; rest content, and you'll find Mr. Biggs cannot be so unfair. Let us give the devil his due, and maybe after all he's not so black as he's painted."

"Sorra a ha'porth myself knows about him,

Father honey, only what old Harry McLean told us. You know Harry went off as a body servant to Sir Charles when he went to the college in England, and he never left Sir Charles while he lived. He came back a few weeks ago and brought a power of news about the new landlord. I heard it all from Tom Moody, the under steward. Harry says Mr. Biggs's mother was a bar-maid in an inn in England. She was very pretty, and Sir Charles's uncle married her; he was the uncle by the mother's side, and as none of the Plover family married, he became the heir. He says these Biggses is all as mane as dirt— savin' your reverence's favor—and that they're good for nothing but psalm singing; his wife is the daughter of some Protestant bishop in England, and they think they're demeanin' themselves mightily to come to live in Ireland at all. They have no one around them but English—barring a head steward, a Scotchman—and sure, your reverence, it's well I know if he's let to have his say in anything it's short Mr. De Courcy 'ill hold the agency, and the likes of him interfarin' between himself and the tenants."

"Mrs. Byrne, my dear child! don't be too ready to believe all you hear. How can you vouch for the truth of what this Harry McLean says; he may have some dislike to Mr. Biggs's family. But now, suppose it all true, those things cannot affect you. Let him manage his household as he likes, that is nothing to the tenantry. As to the Scotchman, it's most probable he is merely a head gardener to look after the demesne. You may be sure he won't have charge of the estate, so don't trouble yourself about it. If you take my advice—and I know you will—go on industriously as you have always done, mind no one's stories, and above all don't repeat them to your neighbors. Keep your children to their lessons and their duties, and never fear. God is good, my dear friends, and we must never forget all He has done for us."

"Och! then, sure its true what your reverence says; glory, honor, and praise be to His holy name we have a great deal to be thankful for, sure enough. And does your reverence really think there's no fear of us bein' put out?"

"Well, my child, I really see no earthly reason why you should be ejected; you always paid your rent punctually, and such tenants as you are a treasure to any landlord with common sense. Now just put such thoughts from your mind and be cheerful at your work as usual. Remember, Kitty, we are always in the hands of God, and He can do as He pleases with us. Walk ever in His presence, my child, and be resigned to His holy will. Don't believe the half of what you hear, Kitty; just let it out at one ear as fast as it comes in at the other."

The cheerful tones of the venerable Father's voice and his smiling face brought comfort to the heart of poor Mrs. Byrne.

She raised her eyes to Heaven, then bowing her head, made the sign of the cross on her forehead.

"Why, then, that your reverence may live long and die happy! I knew I'd get comfort and consolation where I always found it; indeed, Father honey, you took a load from my heart the mornin'."

The priest then led them to talk of other matters—the farm, the stock, the crop, diseases of cattle, etc.; then he came to more domestic matters.

"And so you tell me Andy is makin' great progress at the figures?"

"Yes indeed, your reverence; thanks be to God. Mr. Tobin says he promises to be a fine scholar; he writes a mighty pretty hand, and so does Mike too, for his age, but Winny bates them all at the cypherin'. The master is mighty proud of her, she's so apt at the learnin'. And sure the dacent man has the patience of Job with her; her eye is everywhere to see what mischief she can be at. Th'other night she run the shank of the pipe into the fire til¹ it was almost red hot, just at the time she knew the poor man would be turnin' round to take a draw, and then she put it down mighty cute and slipped out. He took it up by the head, not thinkin' anything, and burned his mouth a little. Another time, she'll be mounted on the ditch with a white sheet about her, to frighten the poor man as he goes home. I do be goin' to kill her, but the father always has an excuse for her."

Father Esmond laughed heartily at Winny's tricks, and told her mother not to be uneasy about her, for she would be a fine girl yet; that it was the lightness of her spirits made her so frolicsome.

Toney and his wife arose to go home, but Father Esmond insisted on their sitting down again. He said they should not stir a step until they eat their dinner with him; that it would soon be ready. So in about half an hour a fine dish of roast chickens and an elegant cut of "belly bacon" reposing on a bunch of young greens, made their appearance on the dining-room table, with crisped potatoes jumping out of their skins, and a tankard of home-brewed ale.

When the cloth was removed, a good glass of punch completed the entertainment. Father O'Toole was in a distant part of the parish attending a sick call.

After chatting awhile, in order, as they said, "not to be like the beggars that run off the minute they get their bit," Toney brought round "the baste," and, both mounting as before, took their departure for home, greatly refreshed both in mind and body.

Father Esmond watched them from the window until a turning of the road hid them from his sight.

"My poor simple children," said he, shaking his head sorrowfully, "God help you, and soften the hardships that are before you. No security for being left in possession of the farm, made valuable by the toil and strength of many an honest man of your name! No hold on the home of many generations but the honor of a Sassenach, and that man the Rev. Samuel Wilson Biggs, the most Papist-hating, smooth-faced hypocrite that ever landed on these shores, and that's saying a big word. God help poor Ireland, and the true children of the soil! Poor Kitty! your heart bodes evil, as well it may, from one of his cloth; but if you only heard all I did, and from such good authority too, of his career in Oxford! My poor, honest, virtuous people! my heart bleeds for them all, but especially for poor Toney Byrne, the last of the once proud chieftains of Wicklow, the O'Byrnes of Glengoulah! Oh, God help us! God help us!"

Thus soliloquized Father Esmond, as with an impatient step and an indignant frown he paced the sitting-room up and down, his hands behind his back.

Suddenly stopping at the table he looked a moment, then drawing over a little stool covered with black cloth, he knelt, and bowing his white head before the crucifix he prayed from his heart out, for patience for himself and his faithful flock, the dwellers of those beautiful hills.

CHAPTER VII.

One fine dry morning in the early part of March, a plain but richly-finished carriage, of a deep shade of chocolate, with linings of crimson satin, drawn by a noble pair of dark chestnut horses, was brought to a sudden stop at the office of Mr. De Courcy by a fat English coachman in clerical livery. The door was thrown open and the step let down in a twinkling by the liveried footman, and out stepped two gentlemen. One was a lean, gaunt-looking individual, with keen, sharp eyes, shaded by shaggy brows, high cheek-bones, and a quantity of sandy-colored frowsy hair. He was attired in a Highland shooting-dress, or something resembling it, and wore a drab felt hat turned up at the ears; his hands and feet were large and clumsy, and his manner ungainly. This interesting individual was Mr. Sandy McGlauren, the head steward of Glengoulah Castle. His companion was a man of low stature, and exceedingly sallow complexion. He had stealthy eyes, which feared to look you full in the face, excepting when worked upon by passion, and then they assumed an expression of fierce malignity; the nose was pinched, and the mouth and chin of a mean receding character. The hair was lank, black, and hung low on the forehead. The dress was plain black, with the exception of the long-tailed white cravat worn by Anglican ministers, and commonly called "a white choker."

His whole appearance bespoke an air of mock humility and sanctimoniousness. He was in fact the very personification of the lowest English mechanic, such as we see so frequently amongst the Mormons who land at the American ports.

This gentleman, it is needless to say, was the Reverend Samuel Wilson Biggs, the proprietor of Glengoulah Castle, and rector of the united parishes of Tinmanogue, Slivedoon, and Kilorglan.

Those three parishes were originally separate, and had each an especial rector; but as they were in the gift of the landlord of Glengoulah, the Reverend Samuel Biggs contrived to remove the incumbents, and very considerately bestowed the whole three upon himself, thereby fulfilling the scriptural adage that "charity should begin at home." Besides this very wholesome reason for retaining the three parishes, the Reverend Samuel had two still more praiseworthy objects in view. First, he knew how very difficult, if not impossible, it would be to find another equally zealous as himself in propagating *his* gospel views—which were of course the only true views; and secondly, he felt the importance of the immense income which those parishes yielded in the form of tithes, in assisting his godly ideas; thus making the mammon of iniquity subserve in spreading the knowledge of the Lord amongst those benighted mountaineers. In the three parishes aforesaid he placed curates at small salaries to do the subordinate work of preaching, giving out service, and attending to the sick—if there were any such who required their presence.

As these two worthies were alighting from the chocolate-colored chariot, a dusty head was stuck out of one of the windows above the office, and the voice belonging to it cried quickly: "Come here, Mick, and look at these quare lookin' customers. Who the D'houl are they at all?" Mick thrust out a head with a paper cap, and a face all besmeared with flour: "Oh, then, swate bad luck to the two of yiz. Yiz are the darlin' pair of turtle doves!" And Mick, fixing his arms akimbo, gazed down admiringly with a comical leer—"That the divil may come jumpin' for the two of yiz; sure that's the ould Scotch haro from the castle, and his psalm-singing master. Throth, I might aisey know 'twas no dacent bodies. Sure it isn't in their skins to look like Christians."

The gentlemen were now shown into the private office by one of the clerks, and the dusty heads disappeared.

Mr. De Courcy came in a few minutes later, and they proceeded to business.

After some conversation about the estate, Mr. De Courcy produced Toney Byrne's lease, and those of sixteen other tenants, all drawn up in legal form, only awaiting the signature of the landlord.

The Reverend Samuel refused to sign, stating as a reason that he considered Mr. McGlauren an excellent judge of the value of land, and he had him go through the farms, examine them, and report upon his observations. His (Mr. McGlauren's) opinion was that the farms were all rented at an absurdly low figure, and therefore he, the Reverend Samuel, had resolved to raise the rents twenty-five per cent., and he wished Mr. De Courcy to signify as much to tne tenantry next rent-day.

A deep flush of indignation passed over the noble features of Mr. De Courcy, and his first impulse was to resign the agency on the spot, but he remembered his promise to Father Esmond, and by a great effort of self-control mastered his anger. His emotion was keenly noted by the sharp eyes gleaming from under the heavy brows of the Scotchman. With a low chuckling laugh, and a shake of his carrotty head, he said: "The Munusther maun be reicht, sir; he maun be reicht" (right). The crimson, but of a paler shade, again for a moment flushed the brow of Mr. De Courcy. Disdaining however to notice the scoundrel, he turned to Mr. Biggs, and represented to him the impolicy of commencing his career in a new country by an act which could not fail to render his name unpopular, not alone with his own tenantry, but throughout the land; reminded him how he came there a stranger, and knew nothing of the wants or feelings of the people; told him how his (Mr. De Courcy's) father had been agent for thirty-five years to that estate, and he himself was close upon twenty-five years, so that it might be supposed he had the best knowledge of the property; and he assured him, if the land had become more valuable, it was because of the untiring industry of the occupiers, who had literally enriched it by the sweat of their brows; that it would be a poor reward for the toil of years to make them pay for their own improvements, and a very poor incentive to others to labor in the same cause.

The Reverend Samuel during this discourse sat

with head on one side, eyes half closed, and hands meekly folded on his breast, like one who had made up his mind to bear all contradictions and trials for the sake of spreading the gospel, for which never-to-be-sufficiently-applauded object he wanted all the money he could scrape together, it mattered not whether injustice, oppression of the poor, ruin of families, or any of those little *minor* circumstances stood in the way—the one grand end had to be accomplished. Therefore, smiling benignly, and casting his eyes up to the ceiling, he said, with an approved nasal pronunciation: "My good friend, I am but a steward in the vineyard over which the Lord hath appointed me. I must do His work; besides, you will please to bear in mind that I do nothing illegal. I do but assert my rights. If those people of whom you speak consider the rent I demand exorbitant, they can give up their farms, and I can find occupiers for them immediately—those, too, who are of the household of the Lord."

"You will pardon me, reverend sir, if I remind you that property has its duties as well as its rights. Let us try to disguise the fact as we may, those poor people are, like ourselves, made from the slime of the earth, and have their human feelings, and human passions too. There is a rule, I believe, which exhorts us to do unto others as we would be done by. A dark, malignant scowl took possession of the godly features of the Reverend Samuel, and his lips became livid; but, quickly recovering himself, this consummate Pharisee arose from his seat, observing,

"Just so, Mr. De Courcy; just so. You have hit upon my principle exactly. You will please notify the tenantry as I told you."

"I must be very dull of comprehension," said Mr. De Courcy, smiling sarcastically, "but I confess I cannot see its application in the present case."

"Ah, my good friend!" and the Reverend Samuel laid his kid-gloved hand blandly on Mr. De Courcy's arm and rolled his eyes upwards, "there are many of the sweetest passages in the book of life, the mysterious meaning whereof is hidden from those who are not called. But be of good cheer and pray; the Lord may vouchsafe to enlighten you yet."

"I must beg to call your attention, sir," said Mr. De Courcy, thoroughly disgusted, "to the case of Anthony Byrne. You surely will not class him with the rest of the tenantry?"

"And why not, pray? Am I under any especial obligations to Mr. Anthony Byrne that I should make an exception in his favor?"

"Well, I rather think you are, Mr. Biggs. Your

ancestors owed the peaceful possession of these estates to the ancestors of Toney Byrne, and you personally owe them your existence at the present hour."

"I do not comprehend you, Mr. De Courcy."

"Know then, sir, that the O'Byrnes of Glengoulah, the direct ancestors of this man, were once the proudest and most powerful chieftains of Wicklow. They were deprived of their estates for no crime but fidelity to the faith of their fathers." The malignant scowl again, speedily succeeded by upturned eyes. "One of those chieftains was a gallant young man. He had just been married when a deed of attainder was sworn against him and his young wife, who was of the Talbot family. His manhood arose against such flagrant injustice, and assembling his tenantry he armed them and fortified the castle in which you now dwell. The roads were not in as good condition as at present, and let me tell you the British soldiery were badly handled at every foray they made upon Glengoulah. Months passed, and still O'Byrne was master of his castle; but the Lord Protector, stung to the quick at the oft-repeated defeats and losses of his men, had ordered a desperate attack to be made on the stronghold the following spring. Poor O'Byrne knew his fate was sealed. He resolved to sell his life dearly, and to die fighting in the sacred cause of home and altar. An unforeseen circumstance changed his determination. During the short cessation of hostilities pending the last attack upon the castle, and whilst O'Byrne and his enemies were both making grand preparations, his wife, the lady Emeline, went to visit a sick tenant who dwelt on the opposite hill. As it was in the morning she deemed no other attendant necessary but her maid. On the way they met two drunken English soldiers, who gagged them, carried them into the city of Dublin, and would have treated them in the most barbarous manner, but a sergeant named Plover just happened to enter the house where they brought the females for concealment. He immediately recognized the lady Emeline as the wife of the chieftain of Glengoulah, whom he had met in many a stormy encounter, and whom he admired for his bravery. With the generosity of a true soldier, he resolved to save her honor at the risk of his life—for in those days it was very dangerous to interfere between a soldier and his prey ; he therefore brought in drugged liquor and treated the miscreants, pretending to applaud their conduct. Soon they slept soundly, and Sergeant Plover carried the lady Emeline and her maid in safety to the castle. The chieftain, in a state of distraction, was with his retainers scouring the hills in search of his beloved wife. They dispatched a trusty messenger to announce to him her safe arrival. On learning from her the noble conduct of Plover, O'Byrne was so filled with gratitude that he consented to surrender without further trouble to the Lord Protector, on condition that Plover was made proprietor of Glengoulah, and he himself permitted to retire to the Continent. The first part of the proposal was gladly acceded to by the Lord Protector, for that castle had cost him already enough of blood and treasure, and Plover was a favorite soldier, having many times distinguished himself by his bravery. O'Byrne, however, would not be permitted to leave the country, but was allowed as a favor to become a tenant farmer on the estate of which he was the rightful lord. This was done to humble his proud spirit, and the gallant young chieftain submitted to his hard fate with the fortitude of a noble Christian soldier.

He tilled his farm with his own hands and the kind offices of his neighbors—once his old retainers, who would insist on helping him, even at the risk of proscription. He thus contrived to make a living for his family.

"Mr. Plover after a while built him a comfortable house, and gave him the farm at a nominal rent.

He would have given it in fee simple, but the law forbade one of his faith to hold property. Mr. Plover in his will left strict injunctions to all his descendants to respect forever the descendants of O'Byrne, and never to harass or annoy them in any manner, particularly specifying how they were indebted to that family for their position in society. The son of this man was made a baronet, and so the Plover family came to possess Glengoulah Castle.

"With regard to your personal affair, Mr. Biggs, your father, the uncle by marriage of the late Sir Charles Plover, was taken a prisoner by the Insurgents in the rebellion of 1798. They had been triumphant in Wexford, and he had papers upon him which convicted him of being a spy for the government. He had but lately come from England on a visit to his brother-in-law.

"He was tried by the court martial of the Insurgents and sentenced to be hanged at daylight next morning. Byrne, the father of the present Anthony, remembering the peril from which an English soldier once rescued one of his ancestors, resolved to save his life. But though he was high in favor with the Insurgent chiefs, he begged Captain Biggs's life in vain; so at all risk he cut the fetters that bound him during the night, and put him in safety on the road to Glengoulah. It was after this occurrence that Captain Biggs married and you were born. The present representative of the once princely chieftains of Glengoulah is now but a peasant farmer; and a more simple-minded, honest man—a more improving, industrious tenant, or a more humble, peaceable Christian, to my mind, does not live on any townland in Ireland than Anthony Byrne. I have his lease here, and you surely will not refuse a request specified in the will of all the Plovers. It is but common justice to the man to whose ancestors, Mr. Biggs, you owe not alone your estates, but your very existence."

The Reverend Samuel Biggs had reseated himself, and it would require the pencil of a Rubens to portray the various changes in his countenance whilst Mr. De Conrcy related the history of the O'Byrnes. One time his cheeks and forehead would turn black as night, and his lips become a livid white with rage; again he would steal a glance at him under his dark brows, and the ferocity of a tiger would gleam from his sinister eyes, but oftenest he kept those visual organs almost closed, and retained his old attitude of Pharisaical sanctity.

The Scotchman remained motionless, and never

once moved his cold, keen eyes from the face of Mr De Courcy.

When that gentleman ceased, his fine open countenance was lit up by the exciting subject on which he had been speaking.

Taking the lease of Toney Byrne from the pile on the table before him, he pushed it with the writing tray towards Mr. Biggs, who, suddenly becoming animated, looked up in his face with a malignant sneer, saying —" My good friend, with all your high eulogisms on this O'Byrne family, it is very apparent from your own showing that they were ever of a rebellious spirit, and disloyal to their lawful sovereign; for if they had been obedient subjects they would have conformed to the glorious Reformation, and thus retained their castle and estates. The loss of their wealth and social position was a just punishment upon them for their disaffection to the constituted authorities. I have no sympathy with rebellion, and shall ever discountenance it."

"And suppose, sir," urged Mr. De Courcy again, "that obedience to the commands of one's sovereign became disobedience to the commands of God, how would you act in that case?"

The Reverend Samuel almost foamed with rage,

while a sardonic fire gleamed from his cat-like eyes. Rising from his chair, he hissed out:

"Sir, you mistake my character altogether. I shall make it my business to find out the disloyal persons on my estate, and get rid of them by all means. I will *never* sign that lease; attend to your orders, sir." Then compressing his livid lips, he stepped into his carriage, followed by the chuckling Sandy, and in a moment they were gone.

CHAPTER VIII.

For a few seconds after they left, Mr. De Courcy stood like one transfixed, looking at the door by which they went out, and which the cautious Scotchman had shut close after them; the veins in his forehead were swollen, and his eyes flashed wildly. Suddenly stamping his boot impatiently on the floor, he drew himself up to his full height, gave his breast a stroke, and exclaimed: "What is the matter with you, Charles De Courcy? Have you become a poltroon, that you, an Irish gentleman of unsullied honor, suffered that upstart English hound to order you? Yes! order me like a hireling?" Making a bound to the door, he touched the handle. It opened, and before him stood Father Esmond, bowing with uncovered head, his white hair flowing behind, and unable to articulate from his labored breathing.

"Oh, my dear venerable friend," said Mr. De Courcy, grasping his hands, and bowing over them to hide his emotion. His passion was all gone now; he was subdued as a child. Leading the old gentleman to the fire he placed him in an easy-chair, roused up a bright blaze, and preparing some mulled wine made him swallow it, with all the tenderness of a son. When the good father was better, Mr. De Courcy said:

"Assuredly it was Providence sent you to me to-day, and just at the right moment too."

"Ah, I understand what you mean. I passed Biggs and the Scotchman as I drove round the avenue to the mills, and he looked black as midnight. I thought immediately there was bad news for my poor flock." Glancing at the table, he said, eagerly, "Has he signed the leases?"

"Indeed he has not, Father Esmond; he refused to do so point blank."

"But Toney Byrne's! He could not refuse to sign his? Tell me that he signed Toney's, and I will rest easy."

"Would that I could do so, Father! There it is, apart from the rest, where I pushed it towards his chair, after making a final appeal towards his sense of justice—*justice!*" he repeated, bitterly; "justice from a Pharisee—a vile, canting hypocrite;" and he flushed to the temples. Arising, he paced the room a few times, then sat down and related the whole substance of his conversation with Biggs, assuring Father Esmond that but for the promise he had made him, and his figure, which seemed continually to rise before him, he would have thrown up the agency, and flung him neck and heels out of the office. "Indeed, Father Esmond, my temper was never so sorely tried in my life."

"Well, God be praised! my dear son; God be praised! It affords me some consolation to think I was any way instrumental in preventing the destruction of my poor people, for if you gave them up they were lost altogether."

"Father, I made you a promise, and I will adhere to it at every cost short of honor."

"Twenty-five per cent. of an increase! Oh, my poor children! My poor children! That's what brought me here to-day. There was a report that the rents were about to be raised. Altogether, goodness knows, they are paying enough; but I never dreamed of anything so monstrous. Twenty-five per cent., Mr. De Courcy! Can any government call itself just which permits one class to hold such power over another?"

"My dear Father Esmond, I have always been conservative in my views, as you know; and as long as the lord of the soil acted with justice and humanity to his tenantry, I deemed it best to take things as they were. But I now see the folly of leaving any class utterly dependent upon another. I could scarcely believe once that any one holding the position of a gentleman could prefer a few paltry pounds to the love and respect of those from whom he derives his income. I have no language strong enough to denounce the British Government if it permits such things to exist any longer. It is a plague spot on its legislation."

"Plague spot! Why, my dear sir, it is robbery of the most barefaced kind. We will suppose a very common case. Give a man a piece of ground, in some cases wild mountain land, which never yielded you any profit; let him toil on it from morn till night, and his sons after him, and their sons again— aye, and their daughters, too; and after generations have ploughed it, manured it, watered it, weeded it, and watched over it with unceasing care and unremitting toil, you inherit it and come a stranger into the country. You say: 'That is a neat farm; how much does that man pay?' 'So much.' 'Ridiculous! That farm would bring much more, and more I will have.' 'But the man in possession made it what it is.' 'What do I care? The law gives it to me, and I only claim my legal rights.' Sir, I respect the highwayman as a far more honorable member of society than that man, for he will candidly tell you he came to rob you; there is no pretence about him. But what shall we say of the law that upholds the scoundrel; not only permits him to violate the first principles of justice, but supports him in the commission of two crimes which cry to Heaven for vengeance—oppression of the poor, and defrauding the laborer of his wages? Now I ask you, if you were not an eye-witness of the fact, could you believe that the boastful and self-styled liberty-loving British Government could perpetrate such enormities in the face of the world in the nineteenth century?"

The old gentleman was fairly out of breath.

"Really, Father Esmond, it never occurred to me in that light before. It is indeed monstrous, and I shall make it my business to have this case brought before Parliament. It is not rightly understood, I think, or those obnoxious laws would be repealed, and more just ones substituted."

"Ha! ha! ha! Justice from the British Parliament! My dear friend, can it be possible you put faith in such a fallacy? I am too old a bird to be caught with such chaff as English legislation. I've seen that tried too often, and always with the same result. God give my poor people patience until He shall send them a deliverer from their intolerable burdens."

"Well, Father, I confess to having some faith still left in British shame, at least, if not in British justice."

"Shame! How long have honest men been trying to arouse their sense of shame to the scandal of making a Catholic people like the Irish support the Protestant Church Establishment, whose doctrines they utterly repudiate? Just think of it: an impoverished, overtaxed people supporting in gorgeous luxury an institution that does nothing for them, either in soul or body! Where is there either shame or justice in that—tell me?"

"Oh, I admit there is no excuse for that abominable tithe system; but you know religious bigotry can transform the most sane man into a fanatic. But here is a subject altogether apart from such feelings—a simple subject of right between man and man. I really think the matter has not been sufficiently investigated and kept before the public; and I do believe if it were, even English legislation would have been shamed into doing justice."

"Well, my son, try it; there is no teacher like experience."

"Pardon me, Father Esmond; I should not have

kept you here so long. Those exciting topics make me neglect good manners. Pray, lean on my arm, sir, and we will go up to the house. Mrs. De Courcy will be charmed to see you."

And so, between chatting with his amiable host and hostess, walking through the gardens and hothouses, viewing the mills and the new machinery, dining and listening delightedly to Mrs. De Courcy singing Moore's melodies, accompanying herself on the harp, it was near eight o'clock of a bright moonlight evening when Father Esmond arrived at his own door, to the great delight of Mrs. Malone, who was in a terrible state of excitement about his asthma, and who immediately commenced scolding him, while she arranged his chair and footstool in the most comfortable manner, and piled the blazing turf. She then transferred herself to the kitchen to scold Pat Lally, his servant man, for "keeping his reverence out in the night air."

We will leave herself and Pat jawing, and take a peep at the poor, benighted people of the town where this good pastor resided, and see how they fared for education.

A short distance from the priest's house, about halfway down the green, was a long, low building, containing rows of benches against the walls on which hung some half-faded maps, boards with simple spelling and reading-lessons for the junior classes, and a couple of black-boards. At the upper end of this apartment was a desk or rostrum to which three steps ascended. Over it on the wall hung a large ordinary colored engraving, in a narrow black frame, of the Crucifixion. On the desk was laid the largest edition of Walker's Dictionary, bearing palpable evidence of having been well used, and a formidable looking cane with a brass ferrule and top. This cane was used with terrible effect *on the sides of the desk* for the purpose of striking terror by its noise, and was a constant companion of its owner on all occasions, save when it rained. In this desk was seated every day a little dumpy man much below the middle size, while the broad shoulders and massive head might have belonged to a pair of legs three times the size of those that bore them. The upper part of the body was evidently intended for a six-footer, but nature in some stingy freak cut the legs short, and so they were forced to expand as best they might, to bear up the ponderous body. Accordingly they did expand broadwise, and a pair of calves like a Dutch Burgher's was the consequence. These calves were encased in spotless white hose with deep ribs, while the feet belonging to them were covered in well-shaped, highly-polished shoes, fastened by steel buckles. The remainder of the costume consisted of a snow-white shirt and cravat, a dark-blue body coat, with bright brass buttons, a pair of breeches of snuff-colored cloth, fastened at the side of each knee by three small brass buttons, a vest of the same material and buttons; a black beaver hat, rather of the Quaker shape, as the leaf was a good deal wider than those usually in vogue; coiled up nicely in the crown of the hat was a clean blue muslin handkerchief with a white vine border; in the fob of the breeches reposed a huge silver watch, which kept time to the second, and pendant from it hung dangling a purple-watered watch ribbon, two inches wide, at the end of which was fastened a large gold seal and key. On a wet or very cold day an overcoat of black freize was laid carefully across the shoulders, the sleeves hanging loose, and a large blue cotton umbrella replaced the cane. This costume never varied once during the lifetime of any one who knew him.

His features were large, strongly marked and coarse; the mouth, a little open, displayed a most independent set of teeth, for each stood on its own merits, with a space between, and as they had no chance for bad companionship they remained untainted to the age of 85. The cheeks were blooming as those of youth, and the head covered with a profusion of coarse hair, which was white as the mountain snow. Such was the personal appearance of Mr. Michael Rafferty, for more than forty years the teacher or "master" of Tinmanogue school. Like most of his class, he was a fine writer, a splendid mathematician, and well versed in grammar, geography, and history, but, unlike many country masters, he knew nothing of the classics.

In repose the face seemed harsh, for the brow was contracted, partly by thought and partly from the habit he had formed of trying to terrify refractory urchins; but when animated, or in conversation he looked up, you noted the gentle expression of his mild blue eye, and your heart warmed to him. Meet him where you would, in the school-house or in the street, morning, noon, or night, Sunday or week-day, he always looked as if he had just made his toilet; his shirt and cravat were always clean, his clothes always brushed, his hat always unruffled, his stockings always spotless, and his shoes ever shining like a looking-glass. It mattered not how wet or sloppy the village streets were, he could manage to navigate through them without a speck. It was a matter of astonishment to all the villagers how on earth he could ever pick his steps in the dark of a winter's morning going to the chapel, back to his lodgings, and then to the school-house, without speck or stain, excepting a very small fringe of mud to the soles of his shoes. Many a one followed him to learn the art, and gave it up in despair, declaring it was a particular knack he had.

And that little dumpy old bachelor (Mr. Rafferty never married), with such an odd figure and coarse features, held one of the noblest and purest souls that ever dwelt in mortal coil. For over forty years he was known to all the inhabitants of Tinmanogue to be in the chapel every morning as the Angelus was chiming six o'clock. Assembling all the poor and whoever wished to join, he recited public morning prayer, read a pious chapter, and then those whose duties would not permit them to stay, went off, and those who could wait remained to hear mass. Amongst the latter was always our venerable friend. After mass he went to breakfast, and thence to school, where he led many a pupil, not alone in the walks of science, but in the more difficult path of Christian perfection. At five o'clock every evening he was again in the chapel reciting for a crowd of faithful souls the Rosary of the Blessed Virgin, and many a fervent Hail Mary went up for the con version of those who strayed from the right path. And who can tell how many wanderers, foot-sore and weary, were brought back to their dear Father's home by the prayers of that humble and faithful band? Here let me remark, in passing, that the last years of this most perfect man have convinced me, more than any other circumstance, that we will have much to suffer for our many imperfections— even the best of us—before we can enjoy the Beatific Vision. He was a little over 85 years of age when he left this world, and I heard those who knew him from his early years—venerable priests who had grown up with him—declare his whole life to be one of most spotless sanctity; his exterior cleanliness, and the neatness with which he picked his steps through the mire, were a type in him (it is by no means always the case, however,) of that interior purity of soul which he possessed, and which brought him unstained through the mire of temptations. Yet, for five years before he quitted this life, he was never able to leave his bed. He lost the use of his limbs, and a most depressing languor fell upon his once stalwart form; but, lying there helpless as a child, the Christian soul rose above this world and its passing sorrows; of him it might be truly said, he lived *on* earth but not *in* it. Every time one of the priests would come to give him the Holy Sacrament he would beg with streaming eyes to be raised to a kneeling posture in the bed, that he might more fittingly receive his Lord and Master as became a sinner.

Light be the turf of holy Ireland on your breast, most dear and venerable friend! I see your every feature before me as distinctly to-day as when a child I sat upon your knee, when you puffed out your cheeks and laughed so joyously when I broke them in with my tiny fists. Many an hour I passed since then in most profitable converse beside that prison bed, yet a murmur never escaped his lips. Many forgot him, as will ever be the case in this world, and sometimes he fared very poorly; but his love, his trust, his every hope, were placed where they ever bear fruit. His only regret was his inability to go to the chapel and be present at the Adorable Sacrifice. Many an effort he made of a beautiful Sunday in summer to arise and creep along by any means, and only gave up the attempt when he sank exhausted, and the good couple with whom he lodged carried him back to bed. For two nights before he died the most ravishing music filled that humble dwelling. Some of the neighbors arose to look out, thinking it was a band returning with excursionists, or from a party at the house of some of the gentry; but the musicians were invisible, and still the entrancing strains filled the air. Upon entering his room next morning (for he always slept undisturbed at night) his landlady, a good, pious woman, who deemed it an honor to wait upon him —as well she might—found him conversing with unseen spirits, his face radiant, she declared; and on calling to him he remained a good while perfectly unconscious of her presence. He afterwards told her the Blessed Mother and her holy spouse, St. Joseph, had been to visit him, and were coming next day at the same hour to take him away. Accordingly, next morning the neighbors were all assembled in his room when they heard him murmur, "Oh, Blessed Mother, I come! Can it be possible!" and his exulting spirit took wing in that glorious company. Who can doubt that myriads of angelic spirits were there attending on the Queen of Heaven, and that they attuned their viewless harps to celestial melody?

Such was the teacher from whom most of the men and boys of Tinmanogue received their education. As might be expected, Father Esmond had a great respect for Mr. Rafferty, and felt well satisfied to have his school under the charge of such a master. Let us now see how the girls fared for instruction. There had long been established in the neighboring town of Ardmore, a convent of the Presentation order, where the ladies devoted their lives to the education of the poor; and where, in addition to the usual English branches, they devoted their attention to straw-plaiting, lace-making, embroidery, and every kind of work, both useful and ornamental. Another convent, of the order of Our Lady of Mercy, had a fine academy for the education of the wealthy, where every accomplishment was taught. For those who could not come into town to school, two male and one female teacher went out giving lessons at the farm-houses through the hills.

One of these teachers, Mr. Tobin, was, as I said elsewhere, engaged by Toney Byrne to visit his farm three times in the week and give, as he expressed it himself, "a draught of his superfluous knowledge from the overflowing fountain of his brain to the young aspirants who thirsted to drink there from." Mr. Tobin was a large-boned man, who walked with a shuffling gait, and always looked as if his bones were thrown together in a great hurry, being left to shift for themselves and get under the skin after their own fashion—and a remarkably funny fashion it was—for he seemed entirely disjointed at every step he took; yet he managed to get over a considerable space of ground in as short a time as most men after all. His garb was what is usually called "shabby genteel." His body-coat, vest and pantaloons were all black *once,* and still had some faint pretentions to that approved shade in gentlemen's wear; his shirt and cravat a dingy white; his hat, a tall thin "stove pipe" with a narrow rim, contained three articles, a brown cotton handkerchief, a small black-covered prayer-book, and a pair of beads, all of the greasiest description. His clothes looked as loosely hung as himself. His head was bald, and his features sharp, as was also his disposition, for all his remarks tended to the sarcastic. Yet, withal, he was a fine teacher and a magnificent penman. Parents deemed themselves fortunate who had engaged Mr. Tobin, and many of the gentry secured his services for their children; but though all respected him for his age and learning, no one loved him; hence the little scruple young people had—your humble servant included—in playing practical jokes on the old man.

The other teacher who shared the labors of Mr. Tobin in the visiting department, was a young man who had been a pupil of Mr. Michael Rafferty. He dressed more fashionably than either of the other masters, and was in fact quite a dandy teacher He knitted his brows very hard and pursed out his lips very much to give himself an air of profound scholarship and determination; but for all his fine clothes and fine airs he lacked the real knowledge of the others, and was consequently little heeded. From this circumstance he was frequently heard to lament the decay of literary taste, and to declare it as "his positive conviction," and no one need try to persuade him to the contrary, "that if a second Byron arose he would not be appreciated in those degenerate days." Such, dear reader, was the state of education in the town lands of Ardmore, Glengonlah, and Tinmanogue when the Rev. Samuel Wilson Biggs, taking pity, in the benevolence of his charitable bosom, on the benighted condition of his semi-barbarous tenantry, determined to carry out a most philanthropic idea which had long lain dormant in that very interesting portion of his clerical form—it was to build a school-house on his demesne, where his sisters could find the most gratifying occupation for their superabundant time, and also earn a well-deserved reputation for sanctity.

The Rev. Samuel, being a man of energy, or, as he would express it, "consumed with the zeal of the Lord," had no sooner matured his plans than he put them into execution; bricklayers, carpenters, painters, and hod-carriers were briskly at work, and by the time the primroses peeped under the hawthorn hedge, and hill and grove had resumed its foliage, an elegant school-house stood in all its grand proportions and all its comfortable appointments.

It wanted but two requisites to make it perfect— a competent teacher, to whom the Misses Biggs would act as assistants when so disposed, and—*scholars*.

CHAPTER IX.

The rent-day came at last, for that is called in landlord parlance, "the spring gale." It was the 25th of March, which every Christian knows is the feast of the Annunciation, and which all the Tinmanogue tenantry knew was a holiday of obligation, even if the bell from the now leafless branches of the elm-tree had held its tongue that day—a crime which could not be laid to its charge, for its clear, sharp tones were carried by the March wind through every glen and ravine of the hills around.

After Mass their venerable pastor read the gospel of the day, and took occasion from it to remark on the life of sorrow, poverty and suffering which their dear Lord had endured on this earth to purchase for them the joys of heaven. He reminded them how sufferings have ever been the portion of the elect, and if borne with that patience and resignation of which their adorable Lord set them the example and united with His bitter passion, they would assuredly bring them all face to face with their Divine Redeemer, who would receive them in

His sacred arms and give them a crown of glory for ever more, in lieu of the short afflictions of this miserable world.

A similar discourse was preached by Father O'Tool to those residing on the townland of Glengoulah, in the little chapel of ease at the top of the hill, and happy was it for those docile children of the Church that their ears and hearts were open to receive those sacred truths from the lips of their pastors; for Almighty God, pleased with their ardent faith and profound resignation, distilled into their hearts the dew of His Divine grace, and gave them strength to bear up with fortitude against the many severe trials which were before them.

After Mass the men all repaired, as was their custom on that day, to the office of Mr. De Courcy, where, as each paid his rent and got his receipt, that gentleman requested him to remain a few minutes, as he had something to say.

When business was over and all had assembled, Mr. De Courcy assured them it was with the utmost reluctance he had to inform all those whose leases had expired, or were about to expire, that their present landlord, the Rev. Samuel Wilson Biggs, had come to the determination of raising their rents 25 per cent., or one-fourth more than they were now paying.

A murmur of discontent ran through the crowd, and many were about to remonstrate and put in their special claims to consideration, but Mr. De Courcy, waving his hand for silence, all was still.

He said, "My friends, you cannot possibly hear this news with more pain than it gives me to tell it; nor can you urge any claim or make any stronger remonstrance against it than I have already done in your name. As long as I hold the agency of this estate I am bound up in your interests, both by duty and inclination, and I know you will believe me when I tell you that if the fortunes of my own children hung upon my words I could not make a more touching appeal than that which I addressed to the landlord, in order to change his intentions; but I spoke in vain. His only reply was, that if any of you think his demand exorbitant, he is satisfied to take the farms off your hands; and, indeed, he said he had persons already in view who were willing to pay the amount he requires. If any of you think you can be more successful than I was by a personal application, I would be very glad you would try it. Those who have no leases will now understand they will have to pay at the advanced rate next September gale, and all the rest as the leases drop. Notices in a legal form will be sent round to this effect. Mr. Biggs has further instructed me to say that he will not sign any lease at present, even at the advanced rate."

Voices now repeated "Long life to you, Mr. De Courcy."

"We're entirely obleeged to *you*, sir, whatever way it turns."

"Sure, well we know it's not your honor's fault," etc., etc.

A report had reached them some days before that there would be "a rise," but they never expected it to be so much; and above all they did not expect to be left without leases.

One fine young man, apparently about twenty years of age, who had a blind father and a paralyzed grandmother to support, now approached Mr. De Courcy, who—concluding he was coming to ask about his lease—said, "He refused to sign your lease amongst the rest, Dempsey."

"Oh, I suppose he did, sir; I did not expect anything else. But will your honor be plazed to tell me did he really refuse to give a lase to Toney Byrne?"

"He did, indeed."

"And did he rise the rent on *him*, sir?"

"He did."

"Well, boys," turning to the other men, "we may

hold our tongues after that! Mr. De Courcy!—I beg your honor's pardon, for I know it's agin your grain to tell such news to us—but I can't help sayin' that's the blackest piece of robbery ever was committed in the County Wicklow. May God defend us all from harm this day!"

"Faix, its yourself is tillin' the truth, Bryan Dempsey."

"Bedad, that's gospel, anyway."

"Och! sure we ought to be ashamed to spake of ourselves at all, so we ought."

These sentences were uttered by several voices at the same time, while poor Toney stood like one transfixed. The news of the raise did not surprise him, for Tom Moody kept Kitty pretty well posted on all such reports as the wily Sandy McGlauren thought fit to put in circulation; nor did Toney care much for that, for his rent was low, and now that he had brought the land into the highest state of cultivation, he could afford it; but the refusal to sign his lease was a blow he never expected. He never spoke or stirred from the spot where he stood till Bryan Dempsey, grasping his hand, drew him into the avenue, where all his neighbors came flocking around him to sympathize with "one of the ould stock," forgetting their own sorrows in the greater one of the lawful heir of Glengoulah. Poor Toney went home to Kitty and the children with sad news and a sad heart. For the first time in his life he was utterly sunk and depressed. Always hopeful until now, he had accustomed himself to look at the bright side of everything, but he had never known before what it was to be dependent upon the will of a landlord, and he felt that the spirit of the Byrnes was broken at last. Still, Toney was a Christian, and high above his sorrows arose his resignation to the Divine will; therefore, though his heart was troubled and his head bowed, he would say: "It's no fault of ours, so welkim be the will of God."

It was plain to Kitty that with all his resignation the light was gone from his heart, and like a true woman she pretended to the greatest hope and courage.

"Tut, tut, man! Don't be a bit afeared. If we have no law itself, he won't put us out while we pay our rent regularly and manage the farm right. Maybe he's only waitin' to see what kind of people we are; and when he knows us better he won't be so black. I'm thinkin' he wouldn't be so bad if it wasn't for that ould Sandy McGlauren. I'm sure he puts wickedness in his head. Well, God is good anyway, and He'll bring us through if all the divils in hell was after us—the cross of Christ be about us, and the protection of His Blessed Mother! Amen!" and Kitty crossed herself and made an attempt at a genuflexion, which was a duck down and a scrape of the left foot behind. When Toney was full of hope six months ago, before the landlord arrived, Kitty was in despair, and could see no gleam of hope whatever; and now, in a sort of affectionate contradiction, because Toney was depressed, her hopes arose. We have seen how she teased her husband night and day until they visited Father Esmond. She now proposed another visit to him for consolation, but Toney decidedly refused to trouble his reverence any more with his affairs. After time had a little blunted the first keen edge of his troubles he worked away cheerfully as ever to all appearance; and since his self-reliant spirit prevented him from intruding his sorrows on his pastor, that old pastor himself, accompanied by his curate, Father O'Tool, drove up in his gig to pay a visit of condolence to Toney and his family. Poor Father Esmond was sadly grieved for the position in which Toney was placed; he told Mr. De Courcy, the day he visited the mills, that he was confident Toney Byrne would be treated with more harshness than any of the tenantry by Biggs, just because he was the rightful owner of Glengoulah Castle. Like all vulgar up-starts, Biggs would hate the idea of coming in contact with a man whose appearance constantly reminded him that he himself was but an usurper. Mr. De Courcy was of the same opinion.

Now, however, Father Esmond spoke hopefully, and begged Toney not to lose heart whatever he did.

Father O'Tool told them so many droll anecdotes that they were in roars of laughter before half an hour passed. The very sight of this fine young priest—who was said to be a lineal descendant of the far-famed royal O'Tools of Glendalough—was enough to revive the most depressed.

He was in appearance "every inch a king." Twenty-eight years old, six feet three "without his boots," and made in proportion; his dark-brown hair fell in shining masses on a noble forehead of alabaster whiteness; his eyes, dark-blue, were dancing with boyish mirth; the nose was a model for a sculptor; the mouth, wreathed in smiles, disclosed rows of pearly teeth, while the cheeks and lips were tinged with the bloom of a happy heart; his carriage and whole appearance was that of a strikingly handsome, noble-looking man, and yet withal there was a simple expression of almost boyish fun and harmless waggery. Wherever Father O'Tool went, there was sure to be a group of children around him. Some swung from his arms, others hung on his skirts, while his voice and joyous laughter were the loudest in the merry throng.

With all his frolicsome ways, no one knew better how to uphold the dignity of his sacred calling, and on the altar, and in the confessional, there was no more zealous and impressive priest. Gathering Toney Byrne's youngsters around him he soon won their confidence, and heard from Mike all the jokes Winnie played on Mr Tobin, the schoolmaster; and Father O'Tool told them in return all the pranks he used to play in his school days. After they had all laughed to their heart's content, he questioned them on their Catechism and other studies, and exhorted them to love and obey their parents. They were sober as judges in a moment, for every child in the parish knew Father O'Tool's habits well: he would be as a child amongst good children, but he became stern as a lion with a sulky or disobedient child; and thus, though they loved him dearly, they very much feared him too. And some children of a larger growth partook of the same sentiments in his regard.

Toney and his wife were highly delighted with the kindness of the good priests in trying to lighten the burden of their trials, and this visit had the desired effect. It kept alive the lamp of hope, and gave them heart to go through their duties, which sometimes of late became irksome as the idea would present itself to their minds that a stranger might be brought in to reap the benefit of their toil. So it was with the other tenantry, the fellow-sufferers of Toney, most of whom repaired to Father Esmond, asking his advice how they should act, and wishing to know if his reverence would recommend them to make a personal application to the landlord. They were all prevented from doing so by the priest, who detailed to them the noble appeal made in their behalf by Mr. De Courcy, and assured them every such application would be met by insult. He consoled them all he could, told them to keep quiet and go on conducting themselves properly, as they had always done, and thus they would disarm the most malicious of their enemies. Those who did not come to him—they were but four, including Toney Byrne—he visited and consoled.

One only man went to the landlord, contrary to the advice of his best friends. He was a fine, stout farmer, named Mat Doran, an upright, honest man, the only support of a blind father, who had lost his sight by a premature explosion in a quarry in which he was working, and a helpless brother who was born an idiot the day after the explosion. As Mat had never injured a human being, and had ever nobly done his duty to all around him, he could not be made to believe that his landlord would be so unjust, and therefore resolved to have a talk with him himself. Giving the knocker a single blow, sufficient to drive a tenpenny nail at least, the door was flung open by a singular specimen of humanity dressed in black livery, with lace epauletts and a powdered wig. He was not by any means the best proportioned man in " that section of country," as a Yankee would say, having a rotund corporation and very slim supporters, set off in fine black silken hose, and low shoes with ponderous silver buckles. The creature was further adorned with blear eyes and a very sallow complexion.

Upon Mat Doran stating that he wanted to see Mr. Biggs, his landlord, upon some business relating to his farm, the powdered lacquey stared at him with his blear eyes in the utmost amazement. "Go and tell him acushla," says Mat, "for the horses is waitin' for me in the field." The footman gruffly slammed the door, leaving the farmer standing out side.

In a few minutes he returned with word that the

Rev. Mr. Biggs never held conversation with his tenantry. He had employed an agent for that purpose, Mr. De Courcy, of the Cascade Mills, and to him he should apply. This message was delivered with all the insolence which could be displayed by a pampered menial. Mat Doran, who had a large amount of waggery in his composition, was determined to have a little fun if he had no justice; he accordingly stepped into the hall, stuck his head one side, and putting his arms on his brawny hips, inspected admiringly the scanty supporters in the black-silk hose, and then the powdered wig. "Beautiful! beautiful!" exclaimed Mat. "I declare to my Kitty, but it makes one strong to see such a fine pair of legs. What do you feed your calves on, allannah? Upon my conscience I'd like to have the resate, for they're the thrivin' pair intirely; you ought to send them to the next cattle show, and you'll be sure to get the pramium!"

The man with the limited understandings was in a rage, and cried, "Begone, you insulting fellow!" But he took care to draw back from the dangerous looking fists of the stout farmer. "Aisey! avic; aisey!" cried the tantalizing Mat. "If you move too fast you'll crack your legs acrass, and sure that 'id be the sin of the world, so it would, for they're the very shape for all the world of a decayed jackass."

"Begone, fellow! I say, instantly!" Mat now burst into a guffaw of a laugh, and made the halls of the castle re-echo with his merriment. "May the divil fly away wid the man that brought you to Wickla; anyway he had a cruel taste for music. Is that the kind of a shape yiz have in England? That I mightn't sin, but if we had such a beauty as you born in Ireland we'd make a fortune exhibiting him. Good mornin', avourneen!" And Mat walked out leisurely, laughing vociferously.

This harmless raillery afterwards cost poor Mat Doran his farm, and threw himself and all he loved on the world.

CHAPTER X.

May " was treading close upon the heels " of June when the school-house was completed. The Reverend Samuel Wilson Biggs, taking counsel with his sisters, came to the conclusion that it would be scarcely safe to spend some hours a day in a building erected so recently; and besides, being so near July, the vacation time, it would not be worth while to open the school until autumn. It was therefore agreed to spend the summer hunting up the right sort of teachers at the lowest rate of remuneration.

The building of the church was progressing rapidly also, and was expected to be ready for service before winter, to the great delight of. Mr. Job Scruggins—the blear-eyed man with the limited understandings—who declared " it was perfectly unendoorable for a gemman to hascend these orful 'igh 'ills every Sunday, not to speak of the natooral disgust a refined pusson must feel meeting so many low Hirish."

The fact was, Job found it no easy task to preserve his equilibrium standing behind the carriage going over Cascade Hill, and as he swung from one foot to another, in order to balance himself, laughing faces peeped at him from cottage doors or mountain bye-paths, and some joke would be perpetrated at the expense of his undeveloped perpendiculars. As Mr. Job Scruggins did not resemble his namesake in patience, he shook his silver-mounted pole at the delinquents in a very threatening manner, a proceeding which was repaid by a shout of derisive laughter from a group of merry urchins who followed the carriage, and one of whom—to show his particular appreciation of the fun—always threw his legs into the air and walked several yards on his hands, head downwards—an accomplishment which he had brought to great perfection by constant practice.

During the summer the Misses Biggs called in their carriage at all the laborers' cottages, to ascertain the number of children in each, and to bear to the hitherto benighted parents the joyful intelligence that "they would soon have an opportunity of having their children educated, as their considerate landlord, ever anxious for their welfare, both here and hereafter, had actually built a school-house for their use, and was about employing a male and a female teacher to impart useful knowledge."

Exchanging looks of commiseration for these ignorant peasants, the ladies drew sighs of profound regret when they found not one single parent prepared to rejoice at the good fortune in store for them.

Some seemed to turn pale at the news. Some said their children went to school to Tinmanogue, others to Ardmore; others again thought their children too small yet; some could not spare them from home, etc., etc. On the fourth day of their unsuccessful canvass, on return to the castle, Miss Rachael expressed her dissatisfaction by declaring she never met such unthankful people in her life. It was her positive conviction they were not a bit pleased to have such a splendid chance to educate their children. She would not be surprised now if they would prefer keeping them at home, or sending them to those old villages with the odious names. Both sisters laughed contemptuously at such schools, " where the pupils are taught nothing but to worship the Virgin Mary, and adore images."

Miss Biggs, in the excess of charity, checked her scorn and reprimanded her sister: " My dear Rachael, we must have pity on those ignorant creatures, bearing in mind how much the Lord hath favored our happy country, where the blessings of His word are so liberally dispensed, and where the population walketh in righteousness. Let us not despair if our footsteps are as yet unmarked by success. We can afford to watch and wait. You know it is written, "For the Lord hath built up Zion, and he shall be seen in His glory." It is a great mark of the mercies of the Lord that he hath vouchsafed to put these unfortunate people into the safe keeping of so godly a man as our reverend brother, and we must even try to arouse him to use his temporal as well as spiritual authority in such a sanctified cause. Be not daunted, my sister; let us go with refreshened hearts to the good work on to-morrow again. Hitherto we have visited only the cottages of the laborers; let us now try the farm-houses, and see what success we may have amongst those of the tenantry *who have no leases.* I fear me we would make but little impression on those who are as yet independent of our reverend brother, for these are a stiff-necked people."

"Well, sister, I will chasten my spirit and accompany you, for your feet seem ever to run in the path of the Lord."

And so day after day the carriage was winding through the hills, ever and anon stopping at the white farm-houses with the trailing vines

The personal appearance of these elderly *young* ladies, barring their rich dresses, was by no means prepossessing; but were they as beautiful as Venus, it would be all the same to the Glengoulah tenantry. The bare sight of them brought heavy grief to many a once happy hearth. Well they now knew why their leases were withheld, and in terror and dismay they fled to their loved pastor for consolation. Poor Father Esmond wept with them, for he saw at a glance the whole map of persecution laid before them, and he could but point to the cross, and exhort them to have courage and patience.

"My poor, poor children!" he would say, while tears coursed each other down his venerable face, "remember the eighth Beatitude: 'Blessed are they who suffer persecution for justice sake, for theirs is the Kingdom of Heaven.' These are the words of our Blessed Redeemer himself, and He wont deceive you. This life is but short after all, my dear people, and soon, oh! soon we shall all meet in our own Kingdom; just think of that. Your dear Saviour tells you that the Kingdom of Heaven is yours! and the Blessed Mother and holy saints will be your companions! and the choirs of angels your musicians! and God himself your most loving Father who will nourish and cherish you for ever more!"

Then there would be sobs and tears of joy and sorrow commingled, until some half-despairing mother would say:

"Oh, Father, honey! I could bear anything myself; but what will I do with my poor children?" And then there would be a chorus of mothers sobbing in sympathy. Thus did this pretended minister of the gentle and merciful Jesus bring wailing and desolation to the homes of those simple, virtuous people.

On the feast of the Assumption of our Blessed Lady, August 15th, Father O'Tool preached a most eloquent discourse to the tenantry in the little mountain chapel of Glengoulah. It was on a Wednesday, and the Biggs school was to be opened the following Monday—a notice to that effect having been sent to all the farm-houses. Everybody was anxious to hear what the zealous young curate had to say on the subject, for they knew he would be sure to give it his earnest attention; therefore the gathering was unusually large, many coming from the townland of Tinmanogue and the adjoining parish of Ardmore. It was a pleasing sight to see groups of people wending their way by so many different roads up the hill to the picturesque little chapel which peeped out at them from a grove, and seemed to smile a welcome as its little painted cross glittered in the sunlight.

Most of the men, the young ones in particular, wore blue body coats with bright brass buttons, yellow or light-colored vests, gray neckties, and well-brushed "Caroline hats," breeches of white or drab corduroy, from the knee of which a knot of the same colored ribbon fluttered in the breeze, while the well-greased pumps and spotless woollen stockings showed off the arched instep and splendidly developed calves to perfection.

The women vied with each other in bright mantles glorying in hoods of quilted silk, and substantial looking bonnets of beaver with gay ribbons, while many of the young maidens wore large hats with flying ribbons, after the fashion of their Welch neighbors across the channel.

Families who lived at a distance came in the well-known low-backed car. Very many of the farmers' wives rode on pillions behind their husbands. Some of the Catholic gentry and wealthy farmers, also shop-keepers from Ardmore, came in jaunting cars and gigs, but the greater number were pedestrians. It was amusing to watch some country swain showing off his horsemanship, the charger being unable to alter from a sling trot if it cost him his life, while his rider rose and fell in the saddle, very much to his own satisfaction, until he gained the side of a group of pedestrians, in the centre of whom was a rural belle equally celebrated for her beauty and her coquetry. It was quite plain, from the smile on her lip, that she knew perfectly well who was reining up close beside her, but she was paying such profound attention to the conversation of a sober-looking young man who walked with her that she never once turned around until the head of the steed, peeping over her shoulder, made her give the prettiest little start and exclamation of surprise.

Just at this juncture a large open carriage dashed by, containing four finely-dressed ladies and two ditto gentlemen, not forgetting the fat coachman and another burly looking gentleman sitting beside him, dressed in black, with a blue satin cravat, in which were jauntily stuck two gold pins with enormous heads, resembling the Lord Mayor's mace, and both fastened together by a slender gold chain. The left hand was partly hidden in a canary-colored kid glove, while the right was uncovered for the evident purpose of displaying a couple of heavy rings; and from the upper vest pocket to the buttonhole, back again to the lower pocket, and then for a quarter of a yard down, hung dangling a massive chain, thick enough for fetters, at the termination of which was a bunch of seals and keys the size of a kitten's head. The two gentlemen seated in the carriage were similarly attired, and sat with their knees touching each other on the outward rim of the cushion to accommodate the four ladies, who reclined back, for the double purpose of seeming at their perfect ease and to make the carriage hold six, whereas it was lawfully intended for four. One of the ladies was an elderly female of rotund figure, good-looking, and dressed as became a staid matron; while the three young ones were bedizened in silks, laces, and jewelry, and were nearly in convulsions of laughter at the costume of the peasantry.

"I do wish you would not giggle so, Beckey," said the matron to the youngest of the ladies, who sat opposite to her; "I know, to be sure, the dress of these here country people is wery haggrawatin', but then we must not forget the big gulf of difference as lies 'atween us, seein' 'ow we 'ad the hadwantage of residin' from birth in a civilized country, while these here poor creeturs never seen nothink but barbarism."

"Well, mother, I can't help a larfin' to save my life. Just look at that old 'oman 'oldin on be'ind the man on 'orse back, with a beaver bonnet and cloth mantle of a 'ot day in Hawgust; if she wouldn't make a dog larf I'll never say nothink again."

"Oh, dear! I shall die of merriment; I know I shall;" said another of the young ladies, who had been gracefully occupied during this conversation in stuffing a cambric handkerchief into her mouth.

"I shall 'ate merriment for hevermore if you do," remarked the young gentleman beside her, giving her a nudge with his elbow, and trying to look tenderly under her bonnet.

"Keep your sharp helbows to yourself, Mr. Scruggins," cried the offended young lady, with an assumption of great dignity.

"I didn't mean hany hoffence, Miss Jenkins," replied the accused; "you are really too hicy cold to an 'art what hadores you." Another nudge and tender glance followed this speech.

"Keep your protestations for them as values them, for I don't." And she cast a look of pitiful contempt on the young lady opposite, who seemed to be carrying on with great gusto a flirtation with her neighbor, and smiling her best at the young farmers as they passed.

"'Old your tongues now, all on you; 'ere we are at the Popish mass 'ouse, and hif they see hany of us a larfin' they wont let us hin." The last remark was made by the matron as the carriage came to a full stop, and the party, trying to look very grave and grand, alighted.

Upon asking an old man with a wooden leg and crutch whether they might go in, he shewed them into a prominent seat on a long bench near the altar-rail—a mark of courtesy to strangers. They immediately commenced staring every one who entered the chapel, lounging for greater convenience on the back of the bench, and twirling their heads in every direction.

As the congregation came in each of them made a genuflexion, often differing in form, and some not the most graceful, but all precious in the sight of God, for whose dear love those faithful hearts bowed in lowly adoration after the fashion their simple minds deemed best. The oft-repeated crossing and genuflexions were a source of much suppressed mirth to the strange party, but when the priest came out in his alb, previous to vesting himself, followed by the man with the crutch carrying a bucket of holy water, into which the priest dipped the asperges and sprinkled the congregation while they remained standing, and the crossing and genuflexions were repeated, a low titter might be heard, which would certainly have broken out and ended by the expulsion of the whole party from the chapel but for the frowns and threatening gestures of the matron, who looked carving-knives at each, and shook her head severely. This matron was the housekeeper of Glengoulah Castle. The youngest of the party, whom she called "Beckey," was her daughter Rebecca, who assisted in her household duties. The other two young ladies were our former fair acquaintances Miss Jemima and Miss Amelia Hopkins. The burly gentleman who sat beside the coachman was Mr. Selling, the head butler. The young gentleman who carried on the comfortable flirtation with Miss Hopkins was Mr. Tompson, "master's hown man;" and the discomfitted young gentleman who was reproved for the sharpness of his elbows, was our friend of the slender supporters, Mr. Job Scruggins, no longer in velvet smalls and silken hose, with a cockade in his hat and a gold-mounted pole in his hand—no longer trying to balance himself on the back of the carriage going over " those villainous 'ills," but dressed like any gentleman, with long trousers of broadcloth, and everything else to match, sitting inside the carriage, and bright eyes smiling around him— and a fair chance to have some fun at the expense of "the wild Hirish," now that his uprights were hidden from mortal vision. A holiday had been given to most of the upper servants on the condition of their first visiting the Popish mass house, in order to bring home the pith of Father O'Tool's discourse regarding the schools; the remainder of the day they might drive through any part of the country they wished, and take a cold dinner with them if they so desired.

Accordingly a well-filled hamper was fastened behind the carriage, and the party, nothing loth, commenced the sports of the day by inspecting the barbarous natives in their house of worship.

Just as Father O'Tool finished hearing some confessions in the sacristy he heard a man inquiring from one of the acholytes if he was disengaged. Approaching the door he saw Tom Moody, who immediately pulled off his hat, and whispering behind it said, "he came to let his reverence know that a carriage had just stopped at the chapel door, and a whole set of the servants from the castle had gone in, with the probable intention of remaining during mass."

"Very good, Tom; I hope they have got a comfortable seat."

"The best in the chapel, your reverence."

"That's right. I am glad they have come; very glad, indeed. I hope they have good memories."

Tom, making a scrape to his reverence, left him to vest and went into the chapel. After the distribution of holy water the Adorable Sacrifice commenced, during which the conduct of the castle people tried the patience of the congregation to the utmost, sneering up in their faces during prayer, nudging and tittering at sight of beads, and staring with ignorant astonishment when the whole congregation were bowed almost to prostration at the ringing of the consecration bell.

CHAPTER XI.

AFTER the communion the priest turned around, read the Gospel of the day, and made a few remarks on the time-honored festival of the Assumption of our Blessed Lady.

He then announced to them that on the Monday following a school would be opened by their landlord, the Rev. Samuel Wilson Biggs, for the avowed purpose of proselytizing the children on the estate.

"Woe to you, people of Glengoulah!" said he, "if, at the bidding of any man—be he landlord, or nabob, or monarch—woe to you! if you place in peril one of those tender souls for which your dear Saviour shed his most precious blood. Your children have hitherto been educated in a manner befitting their station; and, above all, they have been thoroughly instructed in the true faith of Christ—and your venerable pastor has reason to rejoice in his virtuous flock. To God be the glory given! From this, His holy altar, I warn you against the wiles of the Serpent. Remember, you are but stewards placed over the souls of those little ones; your time in this world is but short; and when you depart hence and stand all alone, with God alone as your judge, where will you hide from His wrath when He will demand from you in a voice of thunder, blood for blood? But why do I speak thus? Surely I forget that I am addressing the descendants of heroes! the children of the saints! You well know that every inch of the soil of holy Ireland is watered by the blood of her martyrs, who suffered every species of torture the evil genius of tyrants could invent—the pitch cap, the triangle, the gibbet, impaling upon spears, burning at the stake, tracked by blood-hounds, hunted like wolves, and starved by an artificial famine; but they nobly suffered all and preserved to their descendants the priceless inheritance of the true faith ! It is not *you*—faithful children of those martyred heroes!—it is not *you* who will sell for a mess of such pitiful pottage this magnificent inheritance! this grand old faith! which has stood unchanged for more than eighteen hundred years. Tell your landlord, or his messengers, that in all that relates to the payment of his just demands, you will obey him; but you will not send your children to his schools. You don't want his interference in your family affairs, and you will have none of it. Commit no breach of the peace; but let him under stand, once for all, that he is exceeding the bounds of his duty, and that as you are not exceeding yours you will feel obliged if he will keep to his. It is quite too much for you to support a church in which you have no faith; but to resign to its ministers the education of your children is beyond all endurance, and neither you nor your pastors will permit it."

Much more he said, and in more eloquent language than can be remembered after such a lapse of time. Nearly the whole congregation were in tears, and those who were independent of the landlord were burning with indignation at his conduct. Mass was finished and the congregation dispersed; some to their homes, some to the houses of acquaintances in the neighborhood; while many groups of men, reclining against the ditches or sitting in the grass, held consultation together over the sad aspect of the future. Seated in the centre of the largest of those groups was an old man with a wooden leg and a crutch, who seemed to be relating something of great interest to his auditors, as many who at first reclined on one elbow now sat upright, and leaning their chins on their hands gazed eagerly in his face, now and then giving vent to exclamations of surprise, pleasure, or anger, as their feelings moved them.

"See that, now! Well, glory be to God; but that's fine all out!"

"Bravo, Jerry! be gor its true for yees. Oh, the divil sweep the whole crew of them! Sure its well we know it's not what's right they're studyin'."

"What's right enagh? No! but it's plottin' how they can circumvint the poor, they are, all day long."

"But the brazen-faced lies of them is what kills me: callin' every other nation despots and themselves lovers of liberty."

"Oh, the lyin' divils! Sure they couldn't tell the truth if they tried, so they couldn't."

This wooden-legged old man was Jerry O'Hara, who had served many years in the British army as an artillery-man, had been all through the Peninsular war, and had finally lost a leg at Waterloo, for which he received a pension, and lived comfortably in his native village of Ardmore. Having little to occupy his time, "Lame Jerry," as he was usually called, spent most of his time reading; and, having a retentive memory, he was a perfect oracle among the peasantry, and an ever welcome visitor to their firesides.

Although a most faithful soldier when in service, now that he was out of it Jerry was accustomed to deliver his opinions very freely on the short-comings of the Government, and especially the abominable laws relating to landlord and tenant, and the odious Church Establishment.

In order to strengthen his arguments Jerry hunted up every work which treated on the subject of land tenures in all the countries of Europe, and was quite familiar with the modes of tillage, the products, and particularly the relative positions of landlord and tenant in France, Italy, Switzerland, and Germany. On the occasion in question he was detailing to his listeners, in a high-flown strain of eloquence, the condition of the serfs in Russia, which he had been making his study of late, and contrasting them with the Irish peasantry under the *free* and *enlightened* British Government. "The Russian serf," said Lame Jerry—laying down the case on the palm of his left hand with the two forefingers of his right—" the Russian serf is elevated far in condition beyond the Irish peasant. He never experienced the bitterness of beggary. In his days of misfortune he has not suffered the agony of choosing between the alternative of being separated from every tie of affection, which is next to death, or of dying of starvation. The serf's wife is his wife, and he can keep his vows to her as God has willed it. The serf's children are his children, and he can watch over them from childhood to manhood." (Jerry was probably alluding to the cruel separation of husband and wife, parents and children, in the Government poor-houses in Ireland.)

"In all Russia there is not a single work-house, a single poor-law board, or a single pauper. The cow of the Russian serf is never distrained for rent or taxes. The cabin of the Russian serf is never thrown down unless another is built in its stead. If he is prostrated by sickness, he is cared and tended at the cost of the lord of the soil. If murrain destroys his cattle, or a bad season blights his harvest, the noble has to replace his stock or sow his land. The serf pays no county cess, or poor rate, or income tax; nothing but his obiok or head rent. For this the proprietor gives up his domain to the serfs for cultivation and management. For this he is accountable for their losses and for their support in sickness and in age. And those people are called serfs, and their monarch a despot! And what do you think, but the present emperor is trying his best to free them even from the name of serfs, and give them a right to the land for ever, to be purchased by them in fee simple, if they desire to do so, by installments. Now contrast this country with Russia, and see the difference! You will find the welfare of the people the study of the sovereign in Russia; but show me where you ever found the welfare of the Irish people an object of solicitude to an English monarch? Even the welfare of the English people is a matter of little anxiety to them. In the city of London, where the monarch resides, there is more poverty than in the whole of the Russian empire! The whole aim of the British Government has ever been to oppress the Irish people and squeeze out of them the last shilling; and yet their newspapers are ever lauding the glorious British constitution, and they are particularly eloquent when they come to denounce the shocking despotism of the Russian Czar! So I lay it down as a fact that can defy contradiction, that Ireland, which God made one of the richest countries on the face of the earth, both in agricultural and mineral productions, is the poorest and worst governed portion of the globe, under the thrice accursed British rule." *

A round of applause greeted these concluding sentiments, to which every heart responded, when a noise was heard behind the ditch as of a man leaping down and rustling amongst the hawthorn to disengage himself from its grasp.

---

* Dublin Irishman.

One of Jerry's auditors, a fine athletic young man, catching the branch of a crab-apple tree which inclined somewhat to the road, swung himself on to the ditch and leaned over, just in time to catch the retreating figure of Sandy McGlauren, who was passing over a stile into a neighboring field. The young fellow on the ditch, shaking his fist after him, exclaimed:

"That the divil may come jumpin' for you, and break every bone in your body, for an ould spyin' thief!"

"Who is it, Darby?"

"Arrah! tell us who it is, Darby?" cried several voices, and all started to their feet.

"Musha! Who would it be but that divil of a Sandy."

A chorus of groans followed the announcement, and then a volley of back-handed prayers were uttered in his behalf, many of which consigned him to a perpetual residence in a remarkably warm climate, not forgetting to request that he should be accompanied by his clerical master, as it would be a pity to separate such a lovin' couple; more betoken it would be the sin of the world to spoil two houses with them.

Alternately perpetrating witticisms, making puns,

and praying backwards, at the expense of the unconscious Sandy, the party, with Lame Jerry in the centre, wended their way down the mountain and dispersed to their homes. The remainder of the week was spent by the Misses Biggs in making an especial visit to the farm-houses of the "tenants at will," *requesting* in a most emphatic manner that the will of their reverend brother should be complied with in sending their children to the school he had established for them, *and to no other*. He expected it, they said, and would take no refusal.

Monday came, however, and with it came three pupils—all Protestants. So, as may be supposed, the labors of the male and female teachers, and the Misses Biggs, were not of a very arduous character; indeed, as Sam Weller would say, "it is just possible they could surwive it."

CHAPTER XII.

The day before the September gale (29th) a formal and very stiff note was received by Mr. De Courcy from the Rev. Samuel Wilson Biggs, ordering Mr. De C. to notify the tenantry that his reverence required each and every one of them to send their children to his school, and he would take no excuse. Mr. De Courcy took not the slightest notice of the mandate, and made no observation whatever relating to the school to any of the tenants. He received their rents and gave them their receipts as usual, and they departed for their homes. In a few days afterwards, however, he paid a visit to Father Esmond, showed him the landlord's impertinent missive, and informed him the time had come when he should resign the agency, as he had redeemed his promise, having kept it as long as it was possible to do any good to the tenantry and retain his own self-respect. *That* was no longer possible. And now he had determined to resign it, but would not do so without acquainting Father Esmond.

The venerable old priest at once saw the impossi

bility of any honorable-minded man retaining such an office under such a landlord; and, while he acquiesced in his decision, he gave him many thanks and praises for his great forbearance. "It is happy for me, my dear friend," said the priest, "that your good and respected father so considerately purchased this ground for me, and also my schoolhouse, through his influence with old Sir Thomas Plover, or I too should be at the mercy of this tyrant, and my poor people left without a temple to worship in. And, thanks to your further consideration, you obtained a similar privilege for us from the late Sir Charles, so that we have our chapel of ease on the hill, and no thanks to the present incumbent. May God give us all patience! There will be sad hearts all over the estate when the news of your resignation reaches the tenants. Oh, my poor, persecuted children! my peaceable, happy flock! to be torn by wolves, and worried by hypocritical wretches, with the name of the tender and loving God upon their lips, and their hearts filled with malignity!"

Poor old Father Esmond paced the room, his hands behind his back, and his eyes fixed on the floor, as he gave utterance to these expressions:

"God protect us all! And he calls himself a Christian minister, and writes reverend to his name, and quotes scripture! Oh, God help us! God help us!"

"I am really burning with shame, Father Esmond, as a Protestant, to think such things can be done with impunity by one of our ministers, and we are silent, both press and people. If we only heard of one individual Protestant being persecuted in a Catholic country, what bursts of eloquence would come daily from our press! what vast indignation meetings would be held! what fine speeches made, and flourishing correspondence carried on between the British envoy and the secretary of state! I am thoroughly disgusted with such flagrant injustice. There is no fair play for my Catholic fellow-countryman—I see that very plainly—no liberty of conscience for him. Acts of barbarous cruelty are perpetrated daily upon simple, unoffending people merely because they *are* Catholics. And men—otherwise honorable members of society—are content to shrug their shoulders and wash their hands of it. It sickens me to the soul to see it. As a sincere Protestant, I am determined not to rest satisfied until I get this Biggs disgraced from his sacred office. I believe there is truth and justice still to be found amongst our clergy, and I mean to put it to the test. You smile incredulously, Father Esmond; but I do hope to make my voice heard, both with respect to liberty of conscience and a satisfactory adjustment of the landlord and tenant question."

"Well, God speed you, my dear friend! If you succeed you will confer a priceless benefit on society. I am sure no cause ever had a nobler or more sincere advocate. You will have the most fervent prayers of an old man, though I have not the slightest faith in your success."

The day after this interview Mr. De Courcy's footman left the following note at Glengoulah Castle:

"Mr. De Courcy, having received a very impertinent communication on the 27th September last from the Rev. Samuel Wilson Biggs, wishes to inform that individual that he, Mr. De Courcy, held the agency of the Glengoulah estates under the late Sir Charles Plover for twenty-five years, but he has never yet been agent for a proselytizing institution, nor does he intend lending his services for so vile a purpose.

"Mr. De Courcy further informs the above-named person that from the 29th of said month he has ceased to be the agent for the Glengoulah estates, as he purposes never to have his name connected with any man who has not the instincts of a gentleman.

"CASCADE MILLS, October 3, 18—."

Next morning Sandy McGlauren called at the office for the accounts and documents relating to the estates, which were delivered to him by one of the clerks. And so Glengoulah Castle and estates passed from all honest hands, and the hundreds of hard-working, upright peasantry who dwelt thereon were altogether in the unholy keeping of knaves and tyrants.

Great the grief and loud the lamentations of that once happy tenantry when the intelligence was proclaimed that their much-loved Mr. De Courcy had ceased to be connected with Glengoulah. Tears bedewed every face, and a wail arose from every homestead, such as in Egypt of old awoke Pharaoh from his dream of security when heart-broken mothers and grief-stricken fathers mourned with a great cry the death of their first-born.

The Rev. Samuel Wilson Biggs did not remain long without an agent. He appointed one Jacob Margin as his representative with the tenantry of Glengoulah. He could scarcely have shown a wiser discrimination in his choice, for there never was a more fitting representative of his master, or a more convenient tool to perform any disreputable deed. It will be here necessary to give a short sketch of Mr. Jacob Margin's doings before he was appointed agent for the Glengoulah estates. This hoary old miscreant was both dreaded and detested by every one of his poorer neighbors. Public report said he could not tell who his own father was. It is certain, however, he was of low extraction, for he was brought from a distant county years ago as a land steward to the estate of a Colonel Ranford, an absentee, who had spent his fortune at the Cheltenham Waters in England. Margin arose by trickery until he became agent to the Clonbeggin estate (Colonel Ranford's property), and also to the Bannow Navigation Company, and finally to the mining company of the neighboring district. Having made himself thoroughly acquainted with the state of Colonel Ranford's finances, and finding he indulged in play, Margin strongly advised him to remain in England, representing it as an impossibility that any gentleman could reside in Ireland in consequence of the lawless condition of the people. It was not his fault if this statement were incorrect, for he tried his best to drive the whole country to distraction, and partially succeeded with the Clonbeggin tenantry, and with all the cottiers, laborers and miners who had the misfortune to come under his sway. He had not been more than five years installed as agent to Clonbeggin when Colonel Ranford found himself in very embarrassed circumstances, with an army of duns at his heels. Making some ineffectual efforts to curtail his expenses, he ordered Margin to sell a portion of his unentailed property, and so year by year and bit by bit he sold all his ancestral acres which the law would allow him to dispose of, at an immense sacrifice—the agent declaring it was a most difficult matter to find purchasers, owing to the disturbed state of the country. The colonel then ordered the entailed portion to be mortgaged, and at the end of fifteen years he was so hopelessly involved as to be obliged to fly to the Continent to avoid his creditors. Just at this period his only son came of age, and, in order to check any aspirations after expensive pleasures, the colonel told him the desperate state of his affairs.

Mr. Horatio Ranford, who was blessed with more sense than his father, decided upon starting at once for Ireland, and try to manage the estate himself. We may imagine, but cannot describe, his indignation on finding that Mr. Jacob Margin—or Jab, as he was nicknamed by the peasantry—had been enriching himself at his father's expense. Every portion of Col. Ranford's property which had been sold had been purchased by Margin himself. Every pound which had been advanced upon the mortga ges came from the pocket of Margin at a ruinous interest.

Many a noble tree, too, in the beautiful wood of Clonbeggin, which clothed the hillside overhanging the river Bannow, was cut down and sold, and many more were marked for destruction. Such was the state of affairs at Clonbeggin when Mr. Horatio Ranford arrived from England.

Transported with fury when he discovered the perfidy of Margin, he at once dismissed him from the agency, and immediately employed a lawyer to investigate matters, and, if possible, prosecute the old scoundrel; but the wily rascal had every document so legally drawn up that he defied prosecution, and coolly presented his accounts, showing Colonel Ranford to be £1,500 in his debt. The colonel's estate lay contiguous to that part of the County Wicklow where the coal mines were situated, and, as "Jab" was of a very industrious turn of mind, he took contracts to work them from the mining company. His transactions with this company were worthy the genius of the demon himself. He worked the mines so expensively that for a good while it was all outlay and no return. The company grumbled, became disheartened, and at length stopped the works. To facilitate matters, "Jab" succeeded in damming up the course of a stream which ran by his house, and thus overflowed the whole mines, including the pits on the estate of Lord Wallingford, which extended for miles on the slope of the hill below the water-course.

Upon the plea of removing an evil which he pretended very much to deplore, old "Jab" built a wall around an island in the river, called "Moll Cody's island" (from an old crone who dwelt there alone). It actually belonged to the County Wexford, but "Jab" filled up the stream on the Wicklow side, and deepened the bed of the river behind it, so that the stream changed its course, the island disappeared, or rather became the main land, and formed a portion of the farm of Mr. Jacob Margin.

It was apparently an insignificant addition to his possessions, being only a couple of acres in extent. But of Margin it might be truly said he looked below the surface of things, for his experienced eye saw that a valuable bed of coal lay underneath the island, which he intended to turn to good account. While he protested " the everlasting gratitude of the people was due to him for spending both time and money turning the course of the stream in order to free the pits from water and give employment to the miners, it made his heart ache to see so many hundreds thrown out of work." Notwithstanding all his protestations, however, the water did not move from the pits, and Lord Wallingford's engineers were ungrateful enough to say he did it to enrich himself.

His lordship thereupon commenced a law-suit with Margin for abstracting a portion of the County Wexford contrary to statutes made and provided. He employed barristers of high standing to plead his cause, and, feeling confidence in its integrity, with the calm demeanor of a gentleman he awaited the decision of the court.

Not so his opponent. His course was quite different. Every species of chicanery and fraud, no matter how brazen, was resorted to, provided only he kept clear of the meshes of the law. He had around him a set of sycophants of the most degraded character, and these he employed to serve as witnesses and swear the exact reverse of all that had been proved by the testimony of the other side. What was of still more importance, he had made himself a favorite with the Government for various little services rendered, more easily understood than explained, so that he counted on success as certain, as well he might under the circumstances. The trial came on; and, after various motions and postponements, and finally changing the venue, and going through the whole form again in another county, was twice decided in Margin's favor. All the country people predicted this decision from the commencement, as they said—"Jab was never beat yet, no matter who was against him, for the devil always takes care of his own." Lord Wallingford, becoming disgusted with such low trickery, abandoned the case, and would have no more to do with it.

Now came the turning point in old "Jab's" life —the point for which he had toiled and schemed and planned and robbed with an indomitable energy which should put to the blush those who are striving for an everlasting reward. Few are the Christians indeed who work half so hard for the Eternal Kingdom as this unfortunate wretch worked to gain a position for a few years in this perishable world. He allowed the pits to remain under water about six months longer to save appearances, and the amount of destitution and suffering in the mines was appalling. Hundreds emigrated to America, and hundreds more passed from the earth like shadows, worn out with typhus and various other apparent diseases, but in reality dying by inches from long suffering and hope deferred. Having at length satisfied himself that the mining company were pretty well tired of the mines, Margin laid before them a proposition : it was to rent the whole of the mines belonging to the company at a low estimate, in consideration of the great risk incurred—" which risk, however, he was willing to undertake merely from a benevolent motive to give employment." Out of every £1 which the pits produced he would give them 2s. 6d., or one-eighth.

After pondering on it for a while, and remembering the losses they had already sustained, they agreed to the proposal. A magnificent engine, which cost the company over £3,000, and had long been lying there apparently useless, he purchased from them for £800. To work he went now, and soon the water disappeared from the pits. Men, horses and machinery toiled night and day, and untold wealth was brought up from the bowels of the earth.

CHAPTER XIII.

THIS Margin had a wife the very reverse of himself. A more kind-hearted being never breathed the breath of life, or one more full of sympathy for the suffering poor. This good woman was ever on the watch when her husband's back was turned to see what amount of relief she could distribute. Often would she hide away in a closet the wife of some poor cottier on Jab's unexpected return, and on letting her out through the back gate she would slip a fine cut of bacon under her cloak, in addition to the well-filled bag of meal slung across her shoulder. The fiercer the wind blew or the more incessant the down-pouring rain, the more surely was the excellent Mrs. Margin to be seen straining her eyes through the window-panes, and ever and anon darting out in the storm to look up and down the road, hoping to catch a glimpse of her dear poor, and most lovingly would she take the shivering hands and lead the drenched forms to the warm kitchen hearth.

It is said there is an angel in every house, and

most assuredly there was for a time an angel of mercy under the roof-tree of this incorrigible villain. Many a half-uttered curse was stifled on the lips of the goaded peasantry when they remembered this gentle being.

At a subsequent period, when the people, driven to distraction, formed a secret society, old "Jab" was tried by one of their tribunals and condemned to die for his atrocious robberies and wholesale murders of the poor. A silence for many minutes reigned in that rough assembly, until one gaunt-looking man, with a blackened face and hollow voice, proposed that the sentence should be reversed "for the sake of his wife, the best and kindest woman that ever lived." The motion passed unanimously, and the world was for a while longer cursed by the old miscreant. Margin had two sons and three daughters, nearly all like himself. Besides his own immediate family, he imported a whole colony of nephews from his native county, whom he established in various branches of business. Two had general stores or shops in different ends of the mines, where every article was kept, "from a needle to an anchor." Another was transformed into a doctor, and immediately installed in the county dispensary at a good salary. Another established a mill. One of his sons he made a lawyer. The other, in conjunction with one of his nephews, founded a "Loan Bank," one of the greatest curses ever introduced into a country. This was ostensibly a great accommodation to the miners, as they could borrow small sums, from one to ten pounds, with which they could buy a few loads of coal, and by the sale make a little profit to help in the support of their families. For this accommodation they paid twenty per cent. interest, which was, of course, deducted from the principal before it was paid over. The payments were made by weekly installments, and should be all refunded in twenty weeks. If but one week was omitted there was a fine, and for three the whole was forfeited. Two solvent names besides the borrower's should be on the paper for security, and this document should be laid before the board for a week before the important question could be decided whether the poor, trembling applicant would be refused or not. Many a time the little speculation turned out a failure, or at least did not become available in time to meet the weekly payments, and then the poor wife might be seen trudging her weary way over the hills to the nearest post-town where there was a pawn-office, with her best blue cloak. Next her husband's Sunday frize would go, then their poor bed-covering, until they were perfectly bare. The applicant should first apply to the doctor, making known the amount he required, the purpose for which he wanted it, the names of his securities, etc. If the doctor approved, he would then sign the application, and lay it before the board. They could afterward accept or reject it as they pleased.

For this small act of courtesy the doctor demanded pay—not directly, but indirectly. For instance, he would make it his business to ride past the cabin of such applicant on his way home from the dispensary, and if a clutch of young ducks, or chickens, or a couple of geese, happened to be waddling round, he would call out the poor woman and order them to be sent to his house, stating that he would settle for them with her husband. Woe betide her, however, if she dared ever to remind him of the debt; for her husband or her son would be turned out of the uncle's employment, or their wages cut down, or some species of paltry revenge taken. A few such examples effectually silenced all demands for payment for poultry. The only course left was to hide them; and many a half-naked little boy with bleached hair standing erect as a stubble field, would be perched on a ditch, from which a view of the dispensary could be obtained, watching the door to see which way the doctor's horse would turn. If seen approaching, the poor little urchin would fly like the wind to warn his mother, and ducks, turkeys and all would be driven into the cabin and the door shut, to make believe there was no one in. All the cottiers, miners, laborers, etc., received their pay in orders on the shops, where every article was kept which they could possibly need—of course at a good profit. It was with great difficulty they could prevail upon their task-masters to give them a little money at Christmas and Easter to pay their dues for the support of their clergy. It was a regular habit of the whole Margin tribe to meet at "Jab's" house at stated periods and take counsel together. Each one would then report progress; and if there was a farm that one of them coveted, or a poor cabin formed an eyesore to the landscape from their residences, or any other such trifle stood in their way, all would put their wicked wits to work to find out how they could circumvent the occupiers of such farm or cabin, and then become the owners themselves. Knowing the importance of having a friend in high places, it was their constant study to curry favor with the British Government by denouncing the disaffected, and every other means in their power—a task not at all difficult among a people goaded to madness, and who were often driven to crime from sheer desperation. Thus the Margin family became literally the autocrats of that immense district, so rich in mineral wealth, and the mass of the people held their very existence by the breath of those merciless wretches. Many an unfortunate "small" farmer whose well-tilled fields they coveted, was, by a series of petty persecutions, induced to join the brigade of Captain Starlight, or some other illegal association. His footsteps were dogged by night and day, until he was finally denounced by some of the Margin crew to the minions of the law, and sent to languish out ten or fourteen years in penal servitude, in all probability never more to behold "friends and sacred homes."

As soon as the excitement cooled down, Margin, by some contrivance, would get hold of the coveted fields, and the broken-hearted wife and children would be sent to the road, or worse—the workhouse. One well-remembered circumstance will serve as an illustration for many, many similar ones. A poor, wretched man had been denounced in the way above mentioned and transported. He had never been more than an humble cottier who worked with the neighboring farmers, and who, before and after hours, tried to till one little potato field behind his cabin. The miserable cabin and poor potato patch were, however, painfully visible from Margin's parlor windows, and every expedient was resorted to in order to get possession of them. This poor man's father and grandfather before him had been cottiers, and contentedly tilled the same field and inhabited the same cabin. It was the only home he ever knew, and he loved it as dearly as the rich man loves his ancestral halls; perhaps more dearly, for it was all the world to him. Here he was born; here he was married; and here his seven little ones first saw the light. Margin tried to purchase it, but he would not sell. He then coaxed, wheedled, threatened—all in vain. Thereupon "Jab" commenced to persecute, and a series of petty annoyances—each of which would take a volume to describe—were set to work, until the unfortunate creature was driven to join an illegal society, then in full operation in the neighborhood, and which promised him redress. His was the very voice that begged Margin's life might be spared " for his good wife's sake," while the wretched old villain was tracking his footsteps like a blood-hound. The unfortunate man was discovered with illegal papers on his person, and Margin on the trial represented him as a very lawless character and a disturber of the public peace. He was therefore, of course, sentenced to serve for ten years beyond the seas.

Immediately after his departure a great council of the Margin tribe was held, and the subject under discussion was how to get this cabin out of sight. It might be done eventually by the power of the law, but it would take time; and, as one of the nephews was about to make a very wealthy match, it was quite indispensable to have such an unsightly object removed before the wedding took place. The doctor proposed to take forcible possession, knock it down, and let the wife then go to law *if she could*— a contingency which her poverty made impossible.

This proposition was received with great favor and agreed to be acted upon, but old "Jab" recommended that some weeks should be allowed to elapse until some fresh calamity had abated the public sympathy for this worse than widow and her orphans; and for this purpose it would be necessary to create a kind of panic. Accordingly a false report was spread one morning, about a month later, that Margin's farm-house and mill had been entered and robbed the night before. Many names were mentioned as being suspected, and all were in consternation, for the ukase had gone forth that he would stop all the works for a month if the robbers could not be found—and stopping the employment was the same as a sentence of death to hundreds. Everybody, therefore, was perplexed how to act, and was trembling for his own fate. In the midst of the general confusion a set of strange men, unknown in that part of the country, came from Margin's farm with picks and crowbars to the coveted cabin, and, coolly handing out the wretched furniture, finally dragged out the unfortunate wife and her seven children into the road, pulled off the thatch, broke down the walls, quenched the fire on the hearth, and demolished every vestige of their home; for, however humble, it *was home*, after all, and around it their fondest affections were entwined.

Doctor Margin presided in person over this inhuman transaction—done, too, without even the semblance of a vile law to sustain it. Calling her desolate children round her this heart-broken poor woman knelt down, and, throwing her arms up to heaven, while tears rained down her cheeks, prayed that the wrath of an angry God might descend upon every member of the Margin family—except the one of whom *he* was not worthy—that they might be accursed both in this world and the world to come! It was a terrible scene. Arising, she shook the dust from her feet, and, casting one last look on the heap of ruins she loved so well, she and her miserable little flock took their way with cries and sobs to the house of the parish priest.

The good pastor brought them to his fireside, gave them all the consolation he could, and what temporary relief was in his power. When she told him the curse she had pronounced upon the Margins, he shook his head sorrowfully, and said he regretted she had committed such a sin.

"Father, honey! don't say another word to me!" exclaimed the bereaved creature. "I don't believe that the good and marciful God will ever lay it upon my sowl; because my heart was blistered and He saw it—my good God saw it—and he knows that the same breed tore the father from my poor childer, and I tried to bear it and never cursed them then. But when they tore down my poor cabin, and put out the fire where I had warmed many a desolate craythur for His sake, and when my heart-broken orphans were turned upon the cowld road, I should spake or I'd bust; and I know my blessed Father in heaven will hear my prayer and will never have it afore my sowl. I didn't do it to offind him. Oh, God forbid!" And the poor soul burst into a passionate flood of grief.*

---

* This whole scene occurred exactly as here related.

Mr. Jacob Margin made a smiling garden where this poor home once stood, and beautiful flowers of brilliant hue exhaled their fragrance and opened their petals to the sun, and the birds came there and sang their little hymns of praise, never knowing the bitter sorrow that had wrung burning curses on that very spot from a heart seared with human agony— curses which arose from that broken heart to the throne of the Most High, and which will assuredly, in God's own good time, bear fruit. A few months later it was gazetted that " Mr. Jacob Margin had been appointed to the commission of the peace, his excellency the lord lieutenant having no doubt he would make an energetic and efficient magistrate," and thus the low-born wretch became Jacob Margin, Esq., J. P.

God help poor Ireland!

I would here apologize to my readers for introducing Mr. Margin to their notice. I am painfully sensible he is not by any means a respectable acquaintance. But as we pass through life we must brush against villains sometimes; and as the man lived and figured in many of the sad events recorded in these pages, it is necessary he should be known and his character understood, especially as his nephews and sons are still living, and enjoying the fruits of his knavery. Many a one now in exile through his means, and many who have, thank God! outlived his treachery, will recognize the portrait.

Again I say, God help poor Ireland! and God comfort her oppressed people!

In the long catalogue of the robberies committed upon them by English law—or by Government favorites without any law—there is none so much to be deplored as robbing them of their independent spirit. It is galling to the soul to see them, hat in hand, *craving as a boon* what the meanest serfs in Europe receive as a *right*—namely, *a livelihood out of the soil on which God has placed them.* But it is a thousand times more galling to hear those who ought to know better condemning them for so doing. They cannot help it. Their very lives and the lives of their little ones depend upon their submission to the great man of the district—most frequently a miserable upstart, inferior to themselves in everything but wealth. Many farmers who hold large farms of fine productive land, and who often have money in bank, are afraid to ride a good horse or allow their wives or daughters to appear much better dressed than their poor neighbors lest it should be suspected they had money, for a raise in the rent would surely be the consequence.

The poor cottiers tremble to be discovered with a flock of geese or turkeys, or a litter of young pigs. We have seen from the acts of Doctor Margin how necessary it is to hide them away (unfortunately he has many imitators), and thus the practice of dissimulation is early implanted. Falsehood belongs to the whole system of British rule in Ireland, and is perfectly inseparable from the odious and infamous laws relating to land tenures. Prevarications are essential to the existence of the peasantry under the present order of things. Let those, therefore, who condemn them see if they be not guilty themselves before they cast the first stone at the wronged and friendless poor; and when they hear of some outrage committed by the "Whiteboys," or some such illegal association, let them pause before pronouncing their eloquent denunciations, remembering the intolerable burdens and foul oppressions heaped on the people.

I am not the advocate of secret societies, nor do I believe there is much good affected by them; but it would be well if those who pass such severe judgment on their members would bear in mind that the provocations of the Irish peasant are beyond human endurance, and quite sufficient to excuse his seeking redress after *any* fashion, or to palliate any excess he might commit. They should further bear in mind that no other people under heaven could pass through such a terrible ordeal for centuries, and come out of it with so many shining virtues untarnished.

CHAPTER XIV.

THE grief and consternation of the Glengoulah tenantry was indescribable when they heard that Margin had been appointed agent. *They* knew not what it was to be servile, for they had always been accustomed to being treated by Mr. De Courcy as human beings, whose feelings were worthy of consideration and respect. It therefore took a long time and a well-planned series of persecutions to bring even a portion of them under subjection, while others were driven into rebellion, many of whom were formerly remarkable for their orderly, peaceable dispositions. Margin purchased a small estate as near as possible to Glengoulah Castle, and built a fine house upon it, to which he subsequently removed.

About this time his eldest son, the lawyer—the only one of her children who possessed anything like the heart of his mother—was drowned by the upsetting of a little gig in which he had been taking a pleasure sail on the beautiful Ovoca. The sight of the dead body of her firstborn and favorite son preyed upon the mind of the kind and amiable Mrs. Margin, and she did not long survive the blow.

It is beautifully said, no matter how a man may be debased by sin, he still has some one redeeming trait to show the Divine hand that formed him; "as in a ruined temple, after long searching among the rubbish, one may discover some broken arch or remnant of a once finely-chased capital to mark the finished genius of the architect."* So it was with this most avaricious old sinner. He had one redeeming trait, one green spot in the arid desert of his withered heart. It was a great love for his wife and respect for her virtues, which he would never tire extolling, but would not try to imitate. He mourned her long and sincerely; but sorrow, which purifies most natures, seemed only to stir to its depths the bitterness of his accrimonious disposition. He was a tyrant by nature, and since the only virtuous thing he ever loved was taken from him, he devoted all his energies to the acquisition of his idols—wealth and power.

It is unnecessary to enter into the details of his petty, systematic persecutions, nor would the history be at all edifying. It will be enough to mention that when four years had passed there was a visible

---
* Doctor Cahill.

change both in the farm-houses and the people of Glengoulah. The rents had been increased again and again, until nearly all their hard earnings went into the pocket of the landlord. Then came the agent's "duty work," which means that all the tenants and their laborers are expected to devote some days, turn about, during the season, to tilling his farm free of cost, under pain of his eternal enmity. Add to these troubles the uncertainty of being left in possession after meeting every demand, and wonder no longer that gates were seen hanging by one hinge, cattle roaming at will or grazing in the ditches, pigs and poultry tresspassing upon neighbors, thereby causing disputes and often lawsuits; the cattle pens looking shabby, and the whole byre, once so trim and well-kept, dirty and miry, the poor vines and flower-beds drooping and running wild, the very smoke seeming not to curl up as of old in graceful spiral wreaths, but coming out one time in a sullen gust of indignation, and at another lazily mounting but a little way, and falling back again on the roof of the farm-house with a sad, disconsolate air. The landscape, however, lost nothing of its beauty, for the hand of God had piled the beautiful hills peak over peak, and clothed them with the most exquisite variety of shrubs and trees, and the slopes He covered with the softest and greenest of turf. Then he called out the starry buttercups and daisies to spangle it over, as the blue heavens were spangled at night with the myriad worlds of light; and He filled the groves with bands of feathered musicians; and He commanded the crystal rills to run singing into the valleys, and the brooks, and the birds, and the flowers all obeyed Him; and, therefore, no amount of wickedness on the part of man could mar the lovely prospect.

Well, it is time, after this long digression, to see how Toney Byrne and his family fared in these altered times.

Poor Toney has still the same industrious habits, the same confiding trust in Divine Providence, although there is a great change in his once happy homestead. And death, too, has visited him in the midst of his other cares. His youngest child, Patrick—"the very mott of himself," as his mother used to say—a gentle, good-humored, loving boy, was taken down with scarlet fever, as were Andy and Mike likewise, but the two latter recovered, and little Patrick went to play with the angels and bade adieu to sorrow for evermore. It was a sad trial upon his father and mother to part with this quiet, affectionate little fellow. It was the first child they ever buried, and their grief was great to see him die in the morning of life; but when the first great burst of sorrow had passed, they blessed God for securing their beloved boy a home in His own kingdom, far from the persecutions of their proselytizing landlord and agent. Those three boys had unconsciously brought great trouble to their parents, for they had been continually harassed by messages from the landlord *earnestly requesting* they should be sent to the school designed for them. Toney mildly but firmly refused to send them, alleging "he wanted the eldest boy at home to help him on the farm—the only time he could spare for learning being at night; and as a master came to teach him, why, they might as well all learn together."

Nothing daunted, the Bible-reader of his reverence came again to *request* the two younger ones might be sent.

Not wishing to exasperate his tyrant, poor Toney said "his second eldest boy was inclined to be frolicsome, and he tried to keep him from other boys as much as possible. He would only be a source of trouble in the school, and he did not wish to let him from under his own eye."

A third message came—and this time it was borne by Miss Biggs herself, in her carriage.

"Her reverend brother had sent to *request* the youngest boy to come to school the following Monday morning, as he understood he possessed a very mild temper." Toney was eating his dinner when she swept in awful grandeur into the farmer's kitchen. He told her " his little boy had never been absent from home without some member of his family; and, being of a very timid disposition, he would fret and pine among strangers.

Miss Biggs was very eloquent, and consumed with zeal; Toney Byrne very mild, but determined. All she could get out of him was, that he would wait until the boy grew older before he would send him to school; and he bowed the lady very respectfully into her carriage.

Toney had expressly forbidden Kitty to hold any conversation with those Bible-readers, or any of the Biggs messengers, knowing she would not be able to keep her temper, and would do no good by losing it. Therefore, when they called in his absence, Kitty told them she would tell her husband and let him do as he pleased. Some tried to engage her in a controversy, but she resolutely kept very busy always, and did not remain a moment in the room.

About a year or two after this, just as school opened one vacation, the three boys took the scarlet fever, and the youngest died as we have seen: "a just judgment upon his parents," the Bible-readers and the Misses Biggs said, " for keeping him from the knowledge of the Lord."

His Christian parents took a very different view, however, of his removal. They deemed it a mark of the tenderest love of their dear Father in Heaven to take the gentle child to His bosom, and thus deprive the voracious Biggs of a prey he intended to devour. There was now no fear of his claiming Mike for a pupil, for some months at least, as the minister and his family, like all of their class, had a mortal dread of contagion. So Toney enjoyed about six months' peace.

Winnie still contrived to trail the vines and tend the flowers as of old, for the sake of good Mr. De Courcy, whose gift they were—therefore the farmhouse, in its exterior, looked less changed than most others, but many of its interior comforts were gone. The kitchen roof no longer contained its weighty drapery of flitches of bacon, nor were the bins filled with oatmeal as in former days. Poverty was becoming an inmate where none of God's poor were ever denied relief. But no murmurs nor complaints were heard. Cheerfulness and hospitality still had a shelter around the blazing turf pile, and tales and songs went round; but often the subjects under discussion took a gloomier character than was their wont, and men talked with flashing eyes of the vast change wrought in Glengoulah since Sir Charles died, but especially since old Margin became agent.

The bare mention of the agent's name brought curses to their lips, which were but half uttered when a reproof from Toney stopped them: "Boys, boys, honey! take care what you're sayin' now—don't be sinnin' your souls with him—lave him to God; he can't be worse nor he is, and all your hard words wont make him any better."

"Better eneagh! Be my sowl, he'll be better when the divil has him, but not till thin."

"Well, it can't be very long till that time comes, anyway. Sure the divil has a heavy mortgage on his sowl, and he'll pretty soon be lookin' for his own, plaze the pigs."

"Och! That he may take him body and bones wid all my heart. Don't be shakin' your head at me now, Mr. Byrne; throth its sorry I am that cursin' is a sin, for its fine, manly talk."

"Well, purshume to you! Out of my sight, Tom Moody; you'd make a dog laugh, so you would. Isn't it to pity the unfortunate wretch ye ought? I'm sure, wid all his riches, not one of us would swap places with him, poor as we are (and sure, we could be a great dale worse, glory be to God); would we now?"

"Is it to swap with old Jab? Oh, no! Faix, if we have empty pockets, we have light heels and sound ones too, the Lord be praised!"

This was in allusion to a running sore of long standing which obliged Jab always to appear astride a little, stout-built, black pony, which same animal was often earnestly recommended by passing pedestrians to stumble and break its master's neck—a recommendation, however, the sure-footed little animal heard in dignified silence.

"Well, he can't have very long to run now, himself or his ould leg; let him do his best. There wont be many breakin' hearts after he goes, that's one comfort."

"Be dad, your right there, Peter; for he'll break them all afore he goes, I'm thinkin'."

This last remark was made by Bryan Dempsey, the young farmer who evinced so much sympathy for Toney Byrne the day Mr. De Courcy announced so unwillingly the first increase in the rents, and the landlord's refusal to sign the leases. Little did poor Bryan dream how very prophetic his words were, as far as concerned him and all he loved most dearly. He had become a constant visitor at Toney's farm-house ever since that day, and had endeared himself to every one in the house by his efforts to make them forget their sorrows.

At this present time, however, since the truth must be told, he had a little personal interest to forward there too, for his heart had been attracted to the joyous nature of the pretty, blooming Winnie, now emerging into womanhood. Somehow or other, whatever way it happened, Bryan too had become dearer to Winnie than all the world besides. No doubt it was all because of his great respect for her father. Of course she would not acknowledge such a weakness for any consideration, and was always ready to repel with indignation such a very foolish charge. Nevertheless, a close observer might easily detect how her ear quickened when his visiting hour came in the evening; how her cheeks flushed when a step came into the little porch and the latch was raised; how her heart "fell down into her shoes" when some other head—Tom Moody's for instance—appeared with its "God save all here;" how she tossed her head, looked at the fire, gave a very unnecessary jerk to her spinning-wheel, and had hardly a civil word for poor Tom, who, taking a seat beside her, tried his very best to be entertaining; how another step, and the right head this time, made her pure blood mount to the temples, and how very suddenly she became all attention to Tom's narrative, laughing at his jokes, and asking him many questions, being very careful meantime to avoid the particular spot where Bryan sat.

Yes, indeed, to any observer who knew anything of that mysterious fountain of truest human affection—*a woman's heart*—it was very plain that the teasing, laughter-loving singing-bird of the hills was caged at last. Accordingly, after a little show of resistance on Winnie's part, and many an anxious sigh on the part of Toney, who would fain have seen Bryan's affairs in a more flourishing condition for the sake of his favorite child, as well as for the sake of her brave young suitor whom he loved as a son, Bryan and Winnie were married.

Toney had long since surrendered all hope of leases ever being given by the parson, but he trusted that, seeing how peaceable and industrious they all were, he would leave them in undisturbed possession.

Mrs. Byrne, although she owned Bryan Dempsey to be a great pet of hers, made divers moans at the idea of parting with her only daughter; and although the whitewashed farm-house of Bryan could be distinctly seen about a mile up the hill peeping through the trees from the spot where Mrs. Byrne so often sat spinning, yet she shook her fist at Bryan and called him a "hard-hearted, cruel boy to rob her of her only daughter, her last remaining comfort. She might now sit alone and spin, and who would she have to talk to? Sure all the world and his wife knew boys were not fit companions for a mother," etc., etc.

But the wedding took place nevertheless, and a very pleasant wedding it was too, in spite of their altered circumstances. Nor did the guests find much difference in the quality or quantity of the viands from the memorable occasion six years before when Margaret Byrne was converted into Mrs. Donohoe of Coolanish, County Wexford. The truth was, the same Margaret and her husband, with a thoughtful affection creditable alike to head and heart, came to Glengoulah a few days before the marriage of Winnie, bringing four boisterous young urchins and two or three very suspicious-looking hampers. Now there issued from two of those hampers, I can aver most positively, doleful cries for freedom from several chosen specimens of bipeds which had been kept in durance vile the whole journey, and which, sad to relate, had their heads knocked off on being released from confinement. Certain I am I saw with my mortal eyes the bodies of three gigantic turkeys hanging by the heels at the end of the house, while the perseverance with which the smaller poultry struggled and begged for life was worthy of a better cause. I also received reliable information that a whole sheep and a side of beef were found in concealed parts of the market-wagon on a close inspection. What the other hamper contained must forever remain a secret to outsiders. So

"All went merry as a marriage bell."

Darby Wholahan was there sporting bran new pipes for the occasion, rolling his sightless orbs and making all sorts of grimaces for the amusement of the junior Donohoes and sundry other youngsters who were never done admiring the squeezing of that merry bag of wind, diving every half minute underneath on an exploring expedition to see where the music came from, and always going off in an ecstasy of delight when Darby would make it squeak like a young pig. Ah, but the jigs and reels! You should have been there to see, for my pen fails. "The New Married Bride," "Cover the Buckle," "Hush the Cat," and innumerable others, were done to perfection.

"Now Felix Magee puts his pipe to his knee,
And with flourish so free sets each couple in motion,
With a cheer and a bound lads patter the ground,
The maids move around just like swans in the ocean,

Cheeks bright as the rose, feet light as the doe's,
Now coyly retiring, now boldly advancing—
Search the world all around, from the sky to the ground,
No such sight can be found as an Irish lass dancing."

Well! well! The brightest sun that ever shone upon this world but lends his brightness for a little, and then fades into the deep night. All earthly joys must end; and so the happy wedding-party of Winnie and Bryan was broken up, when, at the dawn of day, the whole company in a body walked up the hill and took a loving farewell of the young couple at the door of the white farmhouse that peeped through the clump of trees.

CHAPTER XV.

A FEW years passed away, the Protestant bishop of the diocese died, and the Rev. Samuel Wilson Biggs was appointed his successor in the Episcopal dignity. It was considered good news by the tenantry on the Glengoulah estate, for they hoped he would remove to the Episcopal palace, where his predecessors always resided, but they were doomed to disappointment.

His newly-created lordship declared it was his intention to reside permanently at Glengoulah Castle. "He could not think," he said, "of abandoning the Lord's pasturage, now that new sheep were daily flocking to feed upon the fatness thereof."

The solution of this mystery was that the storm so long threatening was now about to burst. Notices to quit were served upon every one of the tenants whose leases had expired; and though they did not owe *one farthing* of rent, yet were they all to be ejected from the homes occupied by so many generations of their ancestors. Grief and consternation dwelt in every house. Where were they to turn to? What was to become of their children!

On the townland of Drinimure the tenantry held a meeting among themselves, and discussed the question: "Should their children be sacrificed?" Fear unhappily prevailed over their better judgment, and the agreement come to was that *the children should be given up*. The next day the bailiffs came amid the loud and prolonged lamentations of the parents, many mothers tearing their hair and throwing themselves frantically on the earth. The children were given up, and no more was heard of the ejectment on that townland,* with one exception. No one knew better than his lordship how, for this dereliction of duty, those unfortunate creatures were racked by the bitterest remorse of conscience; and were, of course, most justly excluded by their pastor from partaking of the holy sacraments. Little he cared for the pangs he caused the poor—his paramount determination was to crush the benign influence of the true faith, and to destroy the affection existing between the people and their pastors. Senseless wretch! As well might he try to prevent the green moss from clinging to the changeless rock which supports it, and which it beautifies by its dependent love.

I have said there was one exception on the town-

---

* See the account of the Partry evictions, 1857.

land of Drinimure, which I must relate. A man named Cormac held a fine farm on that townland, and his ancestors before him for more than two hundred years! He was a man proud of his ancient race, whose spirit chafed against these petty transactions. The accession of Biggs to the estate made him rear and plunge like a war-horse, but the appointment of Margin to the agency broke his heart. Every time they came in contact they openly quarrelled, for Cormac never could brook Margin's insolent sneering manner. Happily for poor Cormac, before the expiration of Margin's first year of office he died, commending his widow and only child to God. Mrs. Cormac was a woman of high spirit, and she bravely toiled to keep herself and child in respectability, although the frequent raisings of her rent made it a difficult matter to perform. Her little daughter, Norah, was a sweet child, and went regularly every day to the convent-school of Ardmore, a distance of six miles. Being a talented, amiable child, she was much beloved by the nuns. She had a fine voice, and they taught her to sing many beautiful hymns, and often accepted her services in their choir on festive occasions.

Judge the feelings of this widowed mother when she was called upon *for the last time* to resign her loved and carefully-instructed child, now about fourteen years old, to the care of the Misses Biggs, or give up the time-honored home of the Cormacs forever and become an outcast on the bounty of strangers. Fancy may imagine but no pen could portray the anguish of that mother's heart. Though a young woman, her hair became blanched, and many an hour in the dead of night she would kneel at the foot of a picture of the "Mater Dolorosa," where all the emblems of the sacred passion were represented, lying before the sinless Virgin; again, she would arise and pace the floor, moaning and wringing her hands. Ah, poor mother! who can blame you if for a brief space the tempter triumphed! When the bailiffs entered the house, accompanied by a Bible-reader named Faulkner, Mrs. Cormac fixed her eyes upon them, glaring like a chained lioness; her lips were compressed and her arms tightly crossed upon her bosom, as if to keep them from doing bodily harm to the wretches.

Turning to her child she said, in a harsh, hurried voice, "Go with them, Norah!"

Norah looked wildly at her mother for a moment, and then, uttering a piercing shriek, which never afterward left her mother's ears, she sped down the road like an arrow from a bow, and reaching the banks of the Ovoca flung herself into its now deep and rapid waters, for it was the month of November. Another of the tenants, named Fitzpatrick, who was coming up the road at the moment, saw the action, jumped in and saved her!* He carried her out, and placed her living though senseless form in the arms of her mother, who just reached the spot in a state of distraction. The neighbors helped both to their home. After the application of restoratives the little girl opened her eyes, and seeing her mother leaning over her, clasped her fondly and looked lovingly in her face with a childish smile. The mother was consoled, and blessed God that she was restored to her. Poor soul! she did not then know, what she soon learned, that the dear child, though ever loving and gentle, was an idiot! The light of reason had fled those timid but ever smiling eyes. A few days afterward the Bible-reader called to demand the child again. Norah, shaking from head to foot, cowered behind her mother's chair like a terrified fawn. Mrs. Cormac, confronting Faulkner, exclaimed indignantly—

"Begone, Satan! Tell your hell-hound of a master that I spit upon his notices, and defy his threats!"

---

* "A boy, son of John Fitzpatrick, tried to drown himself rather than be victimized, but was rescued by his father."—From Father Lavelle's Letter on Partry Evictions, 1858.

Seeing the unearthly light that shone in the outraged woman's eyes, the sneaking Bible-reader turned and fled.

The following Sunday night the dwellings of the poor laborers in the town of Ardmore and its neighborhood were invaded by the emissaries of the sheriff, offering the sum of £2 to any man who would assist in the evictions. They met a blunt refusal in many places, notwithstanding the evident destitution under which the poor people were suffering. In one instance a father and his son were offered £4; and another man with two sons was offered £6. Those who have seen the bitter poverty of the poor laborers in Ireland can justly estimate the fortitude and even heroism necessary to refuse such a temptation.

When the recruiting general found he could not succeed he changed his tactics, representing that "they were only required at the castle for a day's little business."

The poor wives of these men, on inquiry, discovered the artifice, and flung themselves on their knees before their husbands, entreating them to reject the bribe. They declared they were satisfied to endure with patience the starvation they and their little ones were suffering, while they had a shelter, even without fire, as they were that cold weather. The men were also offered with the bounty a strong escort of police from the outside of the town until they would return at night, and were told they would be flanked by two divisions of her majesty's 20th regiment, with loaded muskets and screwed bayonets, while they were levelling the houses. The poor fellows said it was not the dread of man that deterred them, but the fear of God, and that they had already too many proofs of the desolation brought on by the accursed *crowbarism* in the neighborhood.*

After some delay his lordship procured ten men, the offscourings of the lanes and alleys of Dublin, to be imported for the work of desolation. On the 26th of November the rain fell in torrents, when there passed through the town of Tinmanogue a body of two hundred mounted constabulary, a troop of infantry, a troop of dragoons, and two pieces of artillery, on their way to the townland of Drinimure to evict therefrom the only evil-disposed tenant on that part of the estate, widow Cormac and her idiot child.

The poor woman had had a succession of fainting fits from the time she discovered her beloved and only child was bereft of reason, and now lay very

---

* See Castleton Papers, November, 1869.—Partry Evictions.

ill. Every exertion had been made by Father O'Tool (who was a kinsman of her late husband), and by Father Esmond, to have this virtuous and injured woman left in her home; but the reverend lord was inexorable. A widow lady who lived a mile or two from this place, but who happily was a tenant to the Dublin Mining Company, brought a car with a feather-bed, protected as far as possible from the incessant down-pour, and placed upon it the dying woman and her idiot daughter. She carried them to her home, and tended them carefully and lovingly as became a Christian, for which may God forever bless her.

Besides the military and police present to overawe the just indignation of an outraged people, Margin was there on his black pony, and his right-hand man, Faulkner, the Bible-reader. A fiendish grin seemed to lurk around the mouths of the vile pair, upon perceiving which Mrs. Dargan, the widow lady above referred to, walked up to Margin and told him whatever might be the fate of Mrs. Cormac, she (Mrs. Dargan) would live to see his power laid in the dust, for she warned him his judgment was not far off.

He laughed scornfully, but her words came literally true. Poor Mrs. Cormac lingered four weeks on a sick bed, and on Christmas Eve her Heavenly Father sent his angels to carry this poor victim of a landlord's intolerance to the throne prepared for her in His own celestial kingdom. Fortified for her journey by the reception of the holy sacraments, and with the venerable Father Esmond giving her the absolution for the dying, she peacefully drew her last sigh.

All day on the festival of Christmas poor Norah watched beside the bed on which lay the silent, wasted form of her loved mother. She would smile and courtesy to the candles, to the crucifix at the head of the bed, and to the neighbors as they came noiselessly in; then, fixing her eyes upon her mother she would sing in a subdued tone a verse from a beautiful Christmas carol taught her by the nuns:

> "God rest ye all good Christians,
> Upon this blessed morn
> The Lord of all good Christians
> Was of a woman born.
> Now all your sorrows He doth heal,
> Your sins He takes away;
> For Jesus Christ our Saviour
> Was born on Christmas day."

No one remembered to have told her it was Christmas day; but with that intuitive knowledge peculiar to idiots she seemed to know and comprehend it all. Might it be that those sinless children of earth, who are debarred from worldly wisdom, being more akin to the angels, derive knowledge from them? Who can fathom? On the feast of St. Stephen, the first martyr, the bell in the great elm tree of Tinmanogue Chapel tolled mournful sounds through the snow-covered groves and ravines of those beautiful hills. How sadly they fell on the hearts of those crowded in small rooms in the villages, who but a few weeks before were the occupants of comfortable farm-houses now levelled with the earth! Not a few wished to be laid to rest in that old familiar graveyard whither the neighbors were with measured tread conveying a widow of the once princely house of Cormac!

Well, to return to the 26th of November.

After the noble exploit of levelling the house of the widow, and driving her and her idiot child upon the charity of the faithful, the great army marched in all the pride of military pomp to the townlands of Drissmore, Tinmanogue and Ardmore. House after house was levelled, and the occupants flung out like weeds on the highway. Two children, sick with the scarlet fever, were carried out by the bailiffs and laid in the ditch with hardly any covering, while their mother, a poor widow, awoke the echoes with her cries. One of them died during the night.

<blockquote>
"Their cot was unroofed, yet they strove to hide
In its walls till the fever was passed:
</blockquote>

> Their crime was found out, and the cold ditch side
> Was their hospital at last.
> Slowly they went to the poor-house and grave,
> But the Lord *they* bent to their souls will save."

Some of the best dwellings and the choicest farms were reserved for the pets of the landlord.

Always desiring to appear humane and merciful while he played the tyrant, Lord Biggs racked his brain to devise some excuse for evicting Toney Byrne, whom he knew the whole country regarded as the rightful owner of those broad acres and that stately castle which he desecrated by his hypocritical presence.

The name of an O'Byrne was hateful to his ears, and he vowed mentally to get rid of the whole "nest of vipers" off the estate. If little Patrick had lived all would be easy enough; but now Andy and Mike were too much grown to go to school, and Winnie's children were too young. What was to be done? He consulted Margin, and that worthy individual came at once to the rescue. He advised his lordship to send Bible-readers to instruct such families as had no children fit for school, and to be guided by their treatment of those "Apostolic men;" "for I think, my lord, with all due respect for your lordship's better judgment, these adults, being (according to nature) nearer their end than the younger ones, require as much, yea, even more, to be regaled and strengthened by 'the Word.'"

"Thou art a very Solomon, my good Margin," exclaimed Lord Biggs in an ecstasy; "it is a most sage advice, and shall be acted upon without delay. Send Faulkner to me."

Margin went off gleefully, rubbing his hands as was his wont when pleased with himself.

Next day Faulkner commenced his labors. He was ordered to go every day to certain families named, and to read and expound for them the Holy Scriptures. Toney Byrne saw immediately the drift of this proceeding. He accordingly took every day to the fields his two sons, and kept them by him. He enjoined his wife to keep her ears stuffed with cotton or wool, and to continue whatever employment she was at, never heeding the expounder.

Things continued thus for a while. But one day Andy complained of feeling sick, and came home from the field about eleven o'clock for the purpose of lying down on the bed.

Faulkner had just finished his exposition and was leaving, when he espied the scapular which Mrs. Byrne usually wore, and which had escaped from her dress. Like a tiger he sprang forward, and, without a word of warning, tore it from her neck.* Mrs. Byrne screamed, and Andy, jumping on the Bible-reader, pounded him until he cried for mercy. Andy then seized his Bible, tore it in flitters, and cast both it and the expounder out of the back door until he landed them on a heap of manure in the pig yard. This sealed the doom of the Byrnes, but Toney never regretted it. He would always avoid quarrels; but when the proper time came for defending the right he was not the one to flinch.

Lord Biggs professed to act with great leniency in not prosecuting the Byrnes after such atrocious conduct, merely contenting himself with dispossessing such evil-disposed, disorderly tenants from his estate.

---
* See Partry Evictions.

CHAPTER XVI.

The sorrow and compassion felt for the Byrnes was greater than for all the other tenantry put together. Loud were the wailings and deep the curses when "notice to quit" was served on Anthony Byrne. A day or two before the arrival of "the crow-bar brigade," every species of vehicle, from Mr. De Courcy's carriage to the market-carts of the farmers on the neighboring estates, and jaunting-cars from the towns around, were tendered to Toney Byrne to convey him and his family away before the bailiffs would come.

His daughter Margaret Donohoe and her husband also came and brought three wagons to convey her parents and brothers, also Winnie and Bryan Dempsey and their little family, to their home—not wishing Margin to have the satisfaction of putting them out. These testimonies of respect and affection deeply touched the heart of Toney, and made his eyes fill to overflowing; but he stoutly refused to be treated differently from the other tenants.

"No, sir; I humbly thank you from my heart

out for your great consideration and wonderful kindness, but I can't accept of it. I am but a simple poor man, like the rest, and if I come of the old stock it is only another reason why I should stand by my people. He is but a sorry captain, sir, that abandons his men in the hour of danger, and it would badly become an O'Byrne to desert the old neighbors."

Such was the substance of Toney's reply to all; and this noble unselfishness but made the wail of grief the deeper when he stepped out in the torrents of rain that chill November morning, leaning on the arm of his daughter Margaret—the rest of the family following in silence, except poor Mrs. Byrne, whose half-stifled sobs were echoed by the women around.

When he got a short distance up the hill Toney stopped, determined to watch to the last the destruction of his home, but it was not levelled. Margin after fastening the windows and doors, put the key in his pocket.

A fortnight subsequently it was taken possession of by Sandy McGlauren, the Scotch steward. Toney and his family were carried by Margaret and her husband to Coolanish, where they were joyfully welcomed by all the Donohoes and their honest neighbors, and where they tried to make themselves useful as possible in their altered sphere. Bryan Dempsey, Winnie, their children, and his blind father and paralyzed grandmother were also evicted in the torrents of rain, and were taken by a cousin of his to his farm some eight miles distant.

Subsequently Bryan Dempsey rented a small cottage and garden in the suburbs of Ardmore, and as he had still left a horse, cart, and a couple of cows, he worked about with the neighboring farmers and kept his family pretty comfortable.

Every one vied in showing kindness to Bryan, for they all loved and respected him for his affectionate attention to his decrepid relatives, as well as for his cheerful countenance and child-like simplicity of character. Winnie, too, was a great favorite, and was as dutiful and respectful to her father-in-law and to old granny as Bryan could desire.

Many of the other tenants opened little shops in the provision line and public houses in the neighboring towns and villages. Many more emigrated to America, where the yellow fever and the malaria of the swamps, where they worked building railways or canals, soon hurried them to the grave.

Oh! if the record of each could only be kept, what a tale it would reveal! But I must narrate the events that befell the Byrnes.

Toney Byrne rented a few acres of land from Tom Donohoe, for he would not live in a state of dependence while able to work, so they got on in peace and virtue, and blessed God for the comforts they enjoyed; but his heart yearned in spite of him for the hills of Wicklow, which were dear to him as beautiful Grenada to the sorrowing Moor, and for the old homestead in Glengoulah, which was his Alhambra.

One night, the first week in January, that same homestead was discovered to be on fire; and while the Scotchman and his family were trying to extinguish the flames in one place it suddenly broke out with even more violence in another and another. And as the wind was in a frolicsome humor that night, he roared up the broad chimneys and danced along the flaming roof, sticking out tongues of flame through the window-frames, and, rolling up the burning thatch, carried off great bundles, letting them spitefully fall in the farm-yard, where the cattle were assembled. He played all sorts of pranks in the hay-loft and stable—going wild with delight when the terrified horses reared and plunged with extended eye-balls. The neighbors came running from all sides, but whether they got suddenly weak at the prospect, or from whatever cause, they gave but little assistance in saving the house, contenting themselves with carrying out of danger the cattle, farming implements, etc., and in preventing the fire from spreading beyond the premises. The flames ceased not until the home of Toney Byrne, from which the poor and the stranger never turned without receiving comfort, was laid in ashes. The pretty garden and flower-beds were trampled under the feet of men and horses, while the beautiful evergreens, the gift of Mr. De Courcy, stood like charred and blackened sentinels presiding over the destruction of the smiling garden they once contributed to adorn.

His reverend lordship turned up the whites of his eyes in holy horror at the depravity of the human heart, declaring he made no doubt it was "that wily Byrne who sent his emissaries to destroy the house he could no longer occupy, and he felt convinced he was instigated to commit the deed by that old priest, who would, of course, give him absolution for it."

The real truth was, poor Toney was almost the only one who did not rejoice when the news spread that Byrne's farm-house was burned, and that Sandy had to find another home.

"Divil's cure to him!" was the invariable response. "He grudged a dacent man the last foothold he had on what belonged to all his generations since the time of the *Phynasians*. He was etarnally stickin' his nose about Byrne's farm, and measurin' the house wid his eye, and he could not speed better bad-luck to all of his sort."

"Be my conscience, then, boys, ye have no raison to rejoice," cried Lame Jerry, "for if ye knew but all, its just what Sandy wanted. Myself thinks as the divil takes care of his own, his black majesty set fire to it to oblige him. Didn't he tell Perry Deacon, the bailiff, in my own hearin', though he didn't see me, that he liked the farm mighty well, but found the house unconvanient; the *ladies* of his family would like a better house."

"Oh! then the divil choke his impudence! The *ladies*, eneagh! Ha, ha, ha! Throughth, its enough to make a dog laugh, let alone a Christian."

"Well, take it aisey now, avic! I'll lay my life Lord Biggs (ahem, God bless the mark!) will be soon buildin' him a fine house to compensate him for the wickedness of these house-burnin' Papists; and ten to one but Margin will be layin' a presentment before the grand jury to levy the expenses off the county as it was the work of an incendiary. Take Jerry O'Hara's word for it, ye'll be made amenable for this crime, and Lord Biggs, Margin and Sandy will put their tongues in their cheek. My friends, they're all *arcades ambo;* but, as ye don't understand Greek, I'll be biddin' ye good mornin'."

We may well surmise that this state of things made secret societies flourish where they never took root before. Nightly meetings were held in churchyards, ruined buildings, and oftenest on the heap of rubbish which marked the spot of a once happy home. Those societies were unknown in Glengoulah during the agency of Mr. De Courcy, while they were in full blast in the neighboring mining districts under the management of Margin.

Now all the evicted tenantry were invited to join them. Many did so, and others refused to have anything to do with midnight assemblies and secret oaths. Among the latter was Bryan Dempsey, who would never listen to their solicitations. As to Toney Byrne, they never even dared to name it to him, his religious principles being too well known.

One night a meeting of this kind was held, and "the Right Reverend Samuel Wilson Biggs, Lord Bishop of Ardmore and Glengoulah by the grace of—Act of Parliament, was indicted before Judge Starlight for the wilful murder of the widow Cormac, the widow Hynes's child, and Peter, Mary and

Bridget Flannigan, besides many, many others, too numerous to mention; also, for depriving Norah Cormac of her reason by brutal treatment in forcing her to attend his proselytizing school, etc., etc."

Witnesses were called and duly examined, but as these cases are already known to the reader it is unnecessary to repeat them here.

The last witness who gave his testimony was Michael Flannigan. He was an old man, with bent form, and hair white as snow. He tottered forward and took from his breast pocket a soiled and torn letter, blotched in many places by the blistering tears dropped upon it. The sight of it sent a shiver through his aged frame, and, as soon as he could speak, he exclaimed:

"Boys, ye all know my fine, manly boy Peter, turned of three and twenty, and my two putty little girls that couldn't brook to see their mother and me in hardship. When we were put out of the ould place they all emigrated to America, lavin' us for a while on my cousin Jack Flannigan's floor. A good friend he ever proved to me and mine—God bless him for it! We were only one week turned out when they went to America. Read this letter; they wrote it to the mother and me from Liverpool."

One of the men stepped forward and read the letter. It was, as usual with Irish letters, brimful of the heart, every second line being dear father and mother: "Don't fret for us, dear father and mother; we are young and strong, thanks be to God for it. We will soon earn a comfortable home for ye both, dear father and mother—a home where old Biggs can't get us, and ye'll end your days in pace, plaze God. Keep up your hearts, dear father and mother; time wont be long passin', we'll soon see one another again. Pray to God and his Blessed Mother for us—we're to sail to-morrow, dear father and mother, in a fine ship called the 'Ocean Spray.' They say she goes a'most as fast as a steamer, and looks grand on the water. God bless you, dear parents; you'll soon hear again, plaze God, from your lovin' children. Till death.

"PETER, MARY, AND BRIDGET FLANNIGAN."

After a few moments the old man, whose head was bowed to his knees and covered with his hands while the letter was reading, rose up again and said, in a trembling voice: "My children never seen the American shore: the ship went down in the Irish say, where she came agin a steamer in a fog, and over four hundred emigrants perished.* My heart's treasures were drowned in sight of the very hills

---

* A fact.

where they were born and played through many a summer day.

"I buried their mother in three weeks in Tinnanogue—her heart broke; and now I'm childless, homeless, and well nigh upon seventy years. If they were left in the ould place, and not forced by a tyrant to transport themselves, my children would be alive to-day; and I now accuse ould Biggs of being their murderer."

"What did he eject you for?" asked Judge Starlight. "Did you pay your rent?" "Yes, to the farthin'; here is my last resate."

"Well, *you* had no child young enough to go to school. I don't see what excuse he had to put you out." "The bailiff told me he said I was a dangerous character, *because I lent Father O'Tool a cart.*" *

Curses loud and deep fell from every lip. Flannigan resumed: "I know an ould man like me, wid one foot in the grave, ought not to be thinkin' of revenge, but I can't help it. I wander over the ruins of my ould home and think I see before me the fire-side, and my children sittin' round it in comfort still; then I start up. And when the wind shakes the trees I think I hear them cryin' and

---
* See Partry Evictions, 1860

strugglin' for life in the dark, deep say! O God pity and look down upon me!" Tears streamed from the old man's eyes, and in that rough assembly, where all were ready for deeds of violence—perchance some already stained with blood—every heart was touched, and many a coarse sleeve was drawn hastily across the eyes. Judge Starlight arose, summed up the evidence, and called upon the jury to decide upon his guilt or innocence. A verdict of guilty was rendered in five minutes. Then the judge in a solemn voice pronounced upon him " the sentence of *Death!*—to be executed at the earliest and best opportunity by some one of the present assembly allotted and sworn for the purpose." Then followed the drawing of lots; and one being appointed, a terrible oath was put to him that, without fear or pity, he would execute that sentence as directed the first opportunity, he being furnished by the society with fire-arms for the purpose.

CHAPTER XVII.

Christmas came with a great fall of snow, the greatest that had been seen for a number of years; but Glengoulah Castle was unusually gay. The lord bishop who ruled there had gone to visit his home in England the previous summer, taking with him her right reverend ladyship and his two sisters.

They returned in time to enjoy the Christmas festivities, and brought with them a large party of fashionable visitors. Among those visitors were two young ladies in the bloom of youth and beauty, nieces of her ladyship. They were the daughters of Sir Harold Menville, of Menville Hall, Middlesex, and their mother was sister to her reverend ladyship. The elder of those girls, though a very estimable young lady, was a stately beauty, and a good deal more worldly than her sister; but Clara was a laughter-loving, mischievous young brunette, all impulse, and with a heart brimful of merriment and kindly feelings. They were enchanted with the lovely scenery, even though the charming hills were covered with snow, and the swollen Ovoca stole darkly and silently along through the leafless groves. There was a dash of romance about their excursions up the mountains that pleased their fancy, and the picturesque costume of the peasantry set them into ecstacies, especially Clara. She loved to go into the farmhouses and cottages and converse with the inmates, especially the children. Soon finding out she was of a different stamp from the Biggs tribe, the women told her and her sister of the many visits paid them by the Misses Biggs to draw them from their faith. Though very indignant to hear it, both sisters made it a subject of amusement to them during their stay. They first complained to their aunt, hoping she would put a stop to it; but they found she was a party in the scheme, and, to their great regret, they were forbidden to visit any more in Irish cottages unless accompanied by the Misses Biggs.

Clara vowed revenge, and never ceased to tantalize the spinster sisters. She would irreverently sing snatches of hymns through her nose; quote all the passages she could hunt up in the Bible which condemned women preachers, and recount for their edification the number of their aristocratic friends in England who had of late embraced Catholicism, and wish she had courage enough to follow their example, as she certainly would before long; not that she had really ever bothered herself on a subject so serious, but just for mischief.

The Misses Biggs, though boiling over, were forced to be silent.

There was to be a grand dinner-party on Christmas day at the castle, and a great ball on St. Stephen's day. Numbers of guests had been invited —some from Dublin—for the occasion; and the castle shone resplendent from the servants' hall to the battlements, from which the "Union Jack" proudly floated.

On the night of Christmas eve the English guests were all assembled in the great drawing-room of the castle. Muffed chandeliers shed a flood of mellow light on the silken hangings of pale amber. Carpets of the softest Persian texture, gorgeous mirrors shaded off with French lace, inlaid tables of inestimable value, and luxurious ottomans, made this noble apartment a fit abode for royalty. Splendid fires blazed in the ample grates of polished steel that stood within mantel pieces of the most elaborate antique carving, each of which was in itself a gem of art. At one of the inlaid tables, in a nook beside the fire, sat his lordship with the Honorable Augustus Kiskdale. Between them was a Chinese chess-board of exquisite workmanship—both were most intent on the game. Dowagers and "men of high degree" played at whist or chatted in groups around the room. A bunch of young beauties were laughing merrily with a troop of young military gentlemen.

Miss Menville was turning the leaves of a scrap-book, which was gallantly held for her by a youthful officer of artillery. Her sister Clara was seated at a magnificent harp, the strings of which she softly swept with a master touch, often stopping to enjoy a burst of merry laughter at the remarks of a stiff, formal-looking baronet, who was turning the leaves of her music and giving utterance to some sombre love speeches of his own peculiar invention. Here was a picture of life, with all its comforts—with all its luxuries.

Without, a wild storm was raging. The wind roared up the chimneys, crashed furiously against the heavy stone casements, and ran tearing and tumbling along the battlements as if meditating the destruction of the whole building. Then would come a lull of ominous import, as if the elements were mustering their forces for a fresh attack. Hark! What's that? A wild gust of snow, sleet, wind, and driving rain, came gushing madly against the shutters of the drawing-room, which however were of great strength and securely fastened, but they could not shut out a blinding flash of forked lightning, followed instantaneously by a tremendous crash of thunder which rocked the castle to its foundations and made the high-born guests turn pale and shiver with fear. His right reverend lordship, who had just captured a "king's bishop" from his opponent, covered his face with his trembling hands.

Another clap and crash on the battlements split the flag-staff through the centre, tore the Union Jack in shreds, and brought down a stack of chimneys in the back part of the building. The ladies gathered in a terrified group around the fire-place near which his lordship sat, excepting the Misses Menville, who quite enjoyed the scene. The mirth-loving Clara fairly danced with glee. "Oh, how grand!" she cried. "Howl on, old storm; I love your music! Oh, for a ramble up the mountains to-night! What say you, Sir William?" she said to her grim admirer, who sat stiff and pale with fright.

A rueful smile lighted up the baronet's face.

"You are full of mirth to-night, Miss Clara."

"Upon my honor I am perfectly serious, sir baronet." And the young mischief dropped him a stately courtesy. "I command you as a true and faithful knight to follow me. Will you? or will you not?"

Before he had time to fashion a reply, sundry screams and the flight of the ladies to the farthest corner of the drawing-room made both turn. The door had been softly opened, and on its threshold stood a slight girlish form with bare and bleeding feet, dressed in a long white gown, her dark chestnut hair flowed down to her waist, and she was perfectly drenched by the storm.

Even Clara for a moment shrank back appalled by the apparition. Advancing into the apartment she seemed to take no notice of the company, but smiled and courtesied to the chandeliers one by one. Just then the great bell in the tower chimed for midnight. All at once she burst forth in a wild sweet voice:

> "God rest ye, merry Christians,
> Upon this blessed morn
> The Lord of all good Christians
> Was of a woman born.
> Now all your sorrows he doth heal,
> Your sins he takes away,
> For Jesus Christ our Saviour
> Was born on Christmas Day.

It was poor Norah Cormac. No one had seen her enter the castle, but she came unheeding the wild elements, and stood face to face with the wretch who had robbed her of home, kindred, and reason

He saw her now by the light of the chandeliers and knew her perfectly. His eyes scowled like a demon's, and he cowered over his inlaid table and shaded his wan face with his hands. Norah heeded him not—she was still smiling, nodding, and conversing with the soft lights shining down on her dripping form.

Clara was the first to approach her. Being satisfied it was no spirit, she at once surmised her to be some poor idiot, and her heart was touched with pity. Advancing toward her she said: "What is the matter with you, my poor girl? You are thoroughly drenched; wont you have some dry clothes and a good supper? Norah again sang her favorite hymn, "God rest ye all," etc.

The ladies were quite horrified when Clara approached the unearthly-looking being, who seemed so unconscious of the presence in which she stood. When they saw, however, how young she was, they began to revive, and her pitiable condition excited their commiseration. Her reverend ladyship rang for the servants, greatly to the relief of her reverend lord, who would have given a goodly sum for the removal of Norah. The servants gathered around her in a group, and their lady ordered them to take her to the kitchen, and to provide her with dry, warm clothes, and a comfortable supper; but the order was easier given than executed. Norah would not move a step for all their entreaties; she had fixed her attention on one particular globe in the chandelier, and kept nodding and speaking rapidly to it in a low tone.

The bishop feared to speak, but he motioned to the servants to carry her off at once. The burley coachman was selected as the ablest, though he exhibited the strongest symptoms of disgust at the idea of lifting that dripping form in his fine clothes. "My heyes!" he exclaimed; "but ain't she wet though? my welvet smalls and silken hose will be utterly ruined! What shall I do?" Hereupon he heaved a deep sigh and made a despairing grab at Norah. In an instant his powdered wig was flying into the fire, and his eyes blinded by a dash of long wet hair. The unfortunate coachman ran for his life down stairs, upsetting the housemaid in his rapid descent, and causing such fright and consternation among the rest of the servants that none of them would enter the room again for anybody's order.

CHAPTER XVIII.

CLARA again approached the maniac girl and said, gently, "My poor child, I wish to be your friend," and she took her cold wet hand in hers; "do come with me to the warm fire, and let me give you dry clothes. Now I know you will come with me," and she tried to draw her gently. Norah was like a lamb in her hands until she moved; but she then resisted, and exclaimed: "Oh, no, no! I could not eat here. I wont have dry clothing! I will never be warm again! Oh! you don't know where I was tonight. When the wind was tearing up the trees, and the thunder crashing as if all the heavens were falling, I was sitting calm and quiet on *her* grave singing! You did not know *her*,—she's gone to God; she died this night, and she always makes me sing that hymn." Here she again sang softly "God rest ye," etc. Clara once more tried to draw her away; but Norah frowned, and again cried: "No, no! Not for all the world would I sit by *his* fire! If I ate a bit it would choke me! She was my mother; and she had no one to love but me. I sat on her grave to-night in Tinmanogue in all the storm, and she bid me come and see him. No one knows how I got into the castle! Ha, ha, ha! I wont tell that; no, no, he'll never know that! Ha, ha, ha! It was he sent her to the grave and left me lonely!" And the poor girl looked so woe-begone up in Clara's face that the young lady's eyes filled with tears. "Who left you lonely, my poor girl?"

"Biggs; old Biggs over there!" and she tossed her head in the direction of the splendid chessboard, whose kings and knights now lay unheeded, for the whole company were listening in breathless silence to the wailings of the young maniac. "He's a bishop now, they say. Ha, ha, ha! He turned her out on the road as cold and as wet a day as this, and she died from it. She bid me come and let him put me out again; and then I'll go home to God. That's what brought me here to-night. He must do it himself; I'll make him! Ha, ha, ha! God rest ye," etc.

"My poor girl, your fears are groundless; the bishop would not harm you." She grasped Clara's arm. "Not harm me? You don't know him. He offered my mother a lease forever of the home owned by the Cormacs for 200 years if she'd sell my soul to the Protestants, but she would not do it for all the gold he has, and he put her out in the torrents of rain in her sick bed. Mrs. Dargan took us both to her house for the love of God, but my mother died on Christmas eve."

"But, my poor child, he would not harm you." Clara's tears flowed down her cheeks.

"I will tell you it was *me* he wanted. Didn't he send Faulkner, the Bible-reader, to bring me along to school? But he couldn't catch me, though. Ha, ha, ha! He chased me; but he couldn't catch me. Ha, ha, ha! When I think of it I laugh 'till I cry again. I thought of it sitting on her grave to-night, and I roared out laughing, only the thunder smothered my voice." The laugh of this poor maniac was perfectly appalling, and made the wretched tyrant shiver with terror.

Norah continued: "Do you know what I did? That lightning flash did not speed quicker through the black heavens to-night than I flew till I got to the river bank, and in I jumped. It was high water too, and I was swept down, down—I don't know any more; and I never could remember anything since. There was always some confusion here" (putting her hands to her temples), "but it all came back to me to-night—the storm brought it all back, and *she* told me how we were dragged out in the torrents from our home. I took a fancy to dress in white always; I think it a pretty dress." (And she looked down complacently at her wet and tattered garment.) "The boys used to call me white lady, some of them; others called me crazy Norah, and all sorts of names, in fun; but they never hurt me." Clara caught at the idea. "Well, Norah, I have a sweet white dress of my own, which I will give you; come, let us try it on, and see if it will fit." Lord Biggs would have given half his estate to be out of the room, but he feared to stir. Now, however, he took the opportunity of the change in her conversation, and was gliding quietly to the door. In a twinkling Norah was holding on to his arm with a death grasp. His teeth actually chattered with dread. "Ha, ha, ha! Old Biggs! did you think you could escape *me?* Do you think I crossed the mountains to-night with torn and bleeding feet, in all the wild storm, to let you off without doing *her* bidding? I'd tear you in bits easier than your bull dog tore my dress, if you didn't do her bidding!" Her eyes gleamed on him with a maniac fire that froze the blood in his veins. "*She* bid me not leave the castle until you put me out in the torrents, as you did before from our home; and then you'll see me no more, for God said he'd take me to His home then. Do you hear me, Biggs?" (And she shook the wretched man with that supernatural strength peculiar to maniacs.

"Come, come on! God's messengers are waiting for me, and *her* bidding must be done."

He looked imploringly around. A young officer made an adroit movement to pinion her arms behind, but she blinded him, as she did the burly coachman, by a slap of her long wet hair.

All drew back in terror. Clara alone seemed to retain her presence of mind.

"Lead her down, uncle," she said; "humor her and when she's once outside I will go with her down the steps and coax her around to the kitchen door."

"Come, come!" cried Norah, clutching his arm; "I can't let you wait." So down he led her to the great hall, followed closely by Clara, who flew into the back hall and secured a couple of cloaks. Her aunt, shaking like one in an ague fit, watched the scene amid her guests from the grand staircase.

Biggs opened the door, and Norah once more singing out—

"God rest ye, merry Christians,"

walked out into the wild storm. Clara was springing after her, but her uncle pushed her back, slammed the door violently, locked it, and then fell fainting to the floor.

In a moment he was surrounded by his sympathizing friends, who raised and supported him to a seat.

Terrific flashes of lurid lightning and crashing thunder now followed in quick succession.

"Oh! God of Heaven! Think of that poor idiot child out in such a storm!" cried Clara; "she will die! Oh! let me follow and save her!"

She ran to the door; but the guests interposed, and her aunt, turning upon her a withering look, exclaimed—

"Miss Clara Menville, I order you to your room instantly. You have made a sufficient fool of yourself to-night."

Poor Clara burst into a passion of tears, and Lieutenant Cordell (the same who tried to pinion Norah) approaching, assured her in a low, rapid voice that he would go out and seek the idiot girl. So Clara was forced to retire to her room.

The young lieutenant was true to his word. Accompanied by a brother officer, and a couple of servants bearing lanterns, they searched the whole demesne and could find no trace of the poor maniac wanderer. They returned to the castle perfectly drenched.

Meantime his lordship was conveyed to his bedroom, where restoratives were administered by his valet. The unhappy man was really sick with terror, and shook on his couch of down like one in a palsy.

Two hours later the wind gradually subsided and died away in hoarse murmurs, and the rain was succeeded by a thick fall of drifting snow.

About four o'clock in the morning every inmate of the castle—which was now dark and still—was aroused by a low mournful cry. It sounded like nothing they had ever heard before; half like the howl of a dog, and half like a human shriek—low in its tones, yet piercing to the very heart. So distinctly was it heard by all that each one fancied it came from some being outside his own window.

A few minutes silence ensued, and, as they listened for a repetition, was heard a faint voice singing slowly—

>"Now all my sorrows He will heal,
>My sins He'll take away,
>For Jesus Christ, our Saviour,
>Was born on Christmas day."

An interval of a few seconds, and the voice again sang slower and fainter—

>"Saviour—
>Was born—on—Christmas day!"

In vain they listened—it was heard no more.

Clara had lain down, but could not sleep for

thinking of the poor maniac, and now she was quite delighted to hear her voice once more.

Arising, she went to the window, softly opened the shutters, and tried to peer out into the darkness. Her window looked out upon the Ovoca, and that enchanting valley " where the bright waters meet."

The dark river, swollen by the late rains, rushed rapidly and silently on; the winds were all hushed, a peaceful calm rested on the lovely hills, while the snow fell in great soft flakes, arraying them in robes of white on that blessed Christmas morn.

Clara closed her window very softly, and stole back to bed. Her heart was comforted to think poor Norah had not been lost in that frightful storm; then her thoughts turned upon the revelations of the maniac girl, and she writhed with indignation and shame to think any of her connections should persecute people for worshipping God in the old faith of Christian Europe; then her thoughts flew back to that very night twelve months ago, when, in the city of London, she accompanied a party of friends of high rank (who had become converts) to midnight mass, and heard in one of those beautiful churches erected by Pugin the grand organ rolling in glorious harmony through the vaulted roof as the choir sang that magnificent hymn that fell from the lips of angels through the golden clouds of morn eighteen hundred years ago:

"Glory to God in the highest, and peace on earth to men of good will!"

Clara's eyes filled with tears and her heart with a new emotion. She resolved to leave no exertion untried to create a new order of things on her uncle's estate, and to begin by hunting up Norah next day and providing everything for her comfort. The great clock of the castle struck five, and Clara, thinking and resolving, fell gradually off to sleep. She dreamed she was again going to midnight mass in London, but she had no carriage as before; the snow fell fast as she found herself traversing alone the sedgy banks of the Ovoca, half blinded by the snow and cutting her feet with the briars and stones. After weary travelling she seemed to reach the church, and a bright light shone around. She listened entranced to the grand choir singing. Looking up she could see no organ, no roof—but soft clouds of translucent light seemed to open, and a troop of angels, with rapturous adoration, sang:

"Glory to God in the highest, and peace on earth to men of good will!"

Watching those celestial forms she was surprised to see that one smiled down upon her who had bleeding feet and a tattered white garment. Gazing at the countenance she recognized the features of the young maniac girl, but her face was now radiant as the sun, and a wreath of glory rested on her long dark hair. Every moment she seemed to grow brighter, and to ascend higher and higher, until the clouds closed beneath her blistered feet and darkness reigned around.

Clara, turning upon her side, fell into a deeper sleep, from which she did not awaken until the great bell rang to summon the househeld to breakfast.

CHAPTER XIX.

Clara's door gently opened, and her maid peeped in.

"I am awake, Palmer," she said; "come along." Emma Palmer came in and busied herself about her young lady, but Clara saw she was troubled by some secret which she was dying to relate. Guessing it to be the supernatural cry which had been heard in the night, she good-naturedly resolved to gratify her. "What's the matter, Palmer?" "Oh, nothing, Miss Clara; I hope you slept well last night, Miss."

"Why, Emma child, you must certainly feel sick, for you are pale as a ghost, and drawing great heavy sighs constantly; are you in any pain?"

"Oh, Miss Clara, I am not in any pain; but I wish we was back again safe in England."

"What are you afraid of, child?"

"Oh, Miss Clara, I feel so nervous; I shall never enjoy nothing in this country any more. They say the castle is haunted; we all heard the most dolefulest cries last night after the rain ceased! I'm sure such sounds never came from the lips of any human creature—it was a most awful cry; then a voice began to sing. Oh, Miss Clara, my heart runs cold—I can't tell you what was found on the front steps of the hall door!"

"Tell me instantly, Palmer; what do you mean?' speak!

"Oh, Miss Clara, don't be angry with me. When the stable-boy went to clear the snow off the marble steps this morning he seed a great pile of snow, as he thought, and took his shovel to it, but could not move it. He called the groom; and what did they find, think you? Oh, Miss Clara, it was that poor crazy girl, frozen to death!"

"Oh, God! Don't tell me she is dead!" cried Clara, springing to her feet.

"Miss Clara, I seed her myself," sobbed Palmer; "she's stone dead."

"Oh God, have mercy on me! Oh why did I not fly to her when I heard her singing—why, why did I let her perish?" And Clara wrung her hands and wept bitterly. "Does the bishop know about this, Palmer?"

"No, Miss Clara; the valet said he was so nervous and frightened last night that no one should tell him; and they sent for a doctor, and the coroner, and the magistrates."

"Who did all this?"

"Mr. Margin, the agent; please you, Miss Clara."

"Well, the bishop *must* be told of it; he has a duty to fulfil. I will go to him instantly, and tell him myself. I do not care for his displeasure."

Away flew Clara in her dressing-gown. Thompson, the valet, opened the door at her knock, and told her his lordship was dressing.

"Well, he wont mind me. I must see him."

She rushed past Thompson and, unannounced, confronted the bishop, who was sitting at his toilet table.

"Oh, uncle! I want to tell your lordship something most important."

For a few moments sobs choked her utterance and large tears rolled down her cheeks.

"Have the goodness to explain yourself, Miss," exclaimed the bishop, in a cold, authoritative voice, which roused Clara's indignation.

"My lord, the unfortunate maniac girl whom you prevented me from accompanying last night lies frozen to death at your door!"

"Well, what if she does? I did my best to shelter and save her, but she was wilfully bent on her own destruction. You were a witness to that yourself."

"No, no! my lord; she would not accept a shelter here, but I could have brought her to some other and saved her."

He pretended not to hear her, and affected composure.

"Thompson, send immediately for Mr. Margin, and let him see to all that is necessary."

"He has been here an hour ago, my lord, and done all you would wish."

"I am much obliged to him. Then let the matter be mentioned to me no more, unless the coroner should need my testimony."

His frigid indifference provoked Clara beyond endurance.

"My lord, my lord; I fear there has been a foul wrong done somewhere."

The face of the bishop grew livid with rage, and the old tiger-light flashed from his eyes.

Thompson withdrew to the outer room, but took care to be in good hearing distance.

"Did you come here to dictate to me, madam? I do not forget your conduct last night. Only for your low propensities, I could have had that pauper instantly dismissed from my presence; but you fostered and encouraged her idle, malicious tales in the very presence of my guests. Yes, madam, to indulge your morbid sensibility, you allowed a drivelling idiot to falsify the character of your own relation, who is, moreover, an elderly dignitary of the Church, and that in his own house."

"It is false! utterly false!" exclaimed Clara. "When the poor victim first spoke of her wrongs I had no idea who her persecutor was. My lord, 'children and fools speak truth,' and I now believe all she said. I also believe the Almighty would not suffer an innocent sheep to perish at the door of the pastor if he were worthy of the name."

She walked indignantly from the room and slammed the door after her like a cannon ball.

Now all his pretended indifference vanished; he shook convulsively, and clutched at the table for support. Wretched tyrant! He writhed under the lash of public opinion, for he drank in those bitter words of Clara: "Children and idiots speak truth."

Well he knew that old adage had passed through more minds than her's; he read it in the faces of his guests in the drawing-room last night, all worldly though most of them were. And now—Oh! that dreaded inquest—the thought was torture. All his long catalogue of extortions and persecutions would become common topics of conversation, and his assumed mask of sanctity would be rudely torn away

Finding himself unable to support those bitter reflections and yet appear calm, he resolved to remain in his room and play the compassionate pastor, overcome by his feelings for one of his lost flock who *would not* be saved. Accordingly Thompson brought him up a dainty breakfast in a service of silver and gold.

About noon the coroner arrived, and a dense crowd of people from town and country. It was many a long day since the noble lawn before the castle was filled by so many honest faces and feeling hearts. Among the rest was the venerable Father Esmond in the carriage with Mr. De Courcy. Although scarce able to breathe, he came with the sympathizing crowd to honor that old branch of the Cormacs. Mrs. Dargan and her son were also there in their jaunting car, with a hearse following behind them containing a handsome coffin and white plumes.

The report had spread like wildfire that Biggs had pushed the idiot girl out in the storm, and that she lay down on the threshold and died of cold!

The coroner, who was an upright man, and anxious to elicit truth, summoned every inmate of the castle to give evidence.

Lord Biggs made a great show of regret at the obstinacy of the crazy girl, declaring that no father could be more anxious for the welfare of his child, but no effort of his or of his household could save her.

The testimony of her ladyship and the guests and the servants followed; but the spectators were little inclined to believe any of them until Clara came forward; and her evidence was given with so much straightforwardness and real feeling that all hearts were inclined in her favor.

When requested by Mr. De Courcy to state if she could account for the idiot girl seeming to feel kindly toward her, yet refusing her proffered assistance, Clara hesitated a moment, and then said—

"The poor child evidently harbored the impression that his lordship had injured her, and nothing could induce her to accept his hospitality, although the bishop was most anxious to have every attention paid her."

Lieutenant Cordell testified to Miss Menville's desire to accompany the girl, and how she had provided cloaks for the purpose, but was prevented by her friends from sacrificing her life on such a terrific night—but that he and Capt. Windham had taken a couple of servants and lanterns and gone over the whole domain without finding a trace of her. The people at the different lodges declared she did not pass through the gates, so he was satisfied she had hidden away somewhere, and that a further search was useless. He said he had no doubt, like many maniacs, she had had a presentiment of her approaching death, and had taken the resolution of dying at the door of one whom (no doubt) her overwrought imagination had deemed her persecutor. Biggs withdrew immediately after Clara's testimony. A verdict was returned of "Death caused by exposure to the cold and wet."

After the verdict was rendered Margin came forward, and said "it was his lordship's wish to have everything regarding the funeral conducted in the most becoming manner and at his expense." A storm of voices replied, "No, no, never! We'll bury her ourselves. We want none of his money!" Here Mrs. Dargan's son came forward, and said his mother had already provided a coffin and hearse to carry her home; and at her house all who respected the house of Cormac could see the remains of the young maniac laid out as became a Christian.

This announcement was received with murmurs of applause—cheers were dispensed with out of respect to the departed. The remains were tenderly borne to Mrs. Dargan's, and having been waked for two nights, according to custom, were carried to Tin manogue on the shoulders of the neighbors—the empty hearse following after—and deposited beside those of her father and mother.

The funeral cortege was the longest seen in that part of the country since the death of Mr. de Courcy's father.

Glengoulah Castle was shut up and the blinds drawn down. His lordship dispatched messengers postponing the festivities indefinitely, and most of the guests departed for their homes.

CHAPTER XX.

The Misses Menville wrote to their father requesting to be taken home. Pending their father's reply the young ladies were scarcely noticed by their aunt and uncle.

Taking advantage of the liberty thus afforded they frequently drove out in a little pony phaeton, accompanied only by a footman. They one day visited the Presentation convent of Ardmore, and were perfectly delighted with the whole establishment, especially the schools attached to it, where the beautiful lace fabrics and straw-plaiting, made by the children, excited their wonder and admiration.

Here was the lie direct given to the oft-repeated tales of the wilful ignorance of the Irish people, and the lamentable darkness in which they were kept by their priests. Both young ladies questioned many of the children on different subjects, and were surprised at the quick intelligence of their replies, as well as their respectful and polite demeanor.

They confessed to each other the superiority in this respect of the Irish peasantry over those of their own country; and could not help contrasting the difference in the mode of education, and the happy looks of the children, with their uncle's false and forced system.

They drew from the superioress the whole particulars of Norah Cormac's birth and education. She seemed at first unwilling to speak harshly of Lord Biggs out of respect to their feelings, but Clara told her what the maniac girl had said about the Bible-reader and their subsequent ejectment from their home, so the superioress then told them the whole truth, and the sorrows and persecutions endured by the whole Catholic population who were under his lordship's dominion. They left a large donation for the schools and returned.

Clara came once again alone. She said her father had written and would be there next day, so they would be leaving immediately for England.

"I came to ask a favor of you, Reverend Mother," she said, blushing deeply. "It is to remember me in your prayers. Mother, I am not happy; my mind is not at rest;" and her eyes filled with tears, as did those of the good mother.

"My dear young lady, calm yourself," she replied; "I feel assured you are very dear to the sacred heart of Jesus, and that he has great designs on your soul. We have anticipated your wishes already, dear child, and daily recite a bead for you and your sister, to whose generosity we are so much indebted; but we will say additional prayers for you especially for the future. And now I want you to confer a small favor on me in return."

As she spoke she unlocked an escritoire which stood in a recess, and took from one of the compartments a gold medal of Mary Immaculate. Presenting it to Clara, she said: "Now promise me, dear young lady, to wear this constantly, and daily recite one 'Hail Mary' for light to guide you to the right path." Do not let sneers or frowns deter you from wearing this holy medal, which is blessed in the Catholic Church, remembering the words of Scripture—'Every creature of God is good, and nothing to be rejected that is received with thanksgiving, for it is sanctified by the word of God and prayer.'

"Should any of your friends laugh at you for venerating a bit of metal, remind them how the Israelites were cured of a venomous bite by looking on a piece of metal made in the form of a serpent."

Clara, sobbing, promised faithfully to fulfil the request of the nun.

The superioress embraced her warmly and they parted.

The following year Clara had the happiness to become acquainted in London with dear Father Faber —the very angel of converts—and under his spiritual guidance she, with the consent of her father, entered the *one* sheepfold of the *one* shepherd!

The death of Norah Cormac, under such circumstances, did not serve to increase the popularity of Biggs—he became more obnoxious than ever; and, as if to defy public opinion still more, he showed his petty malignity by impounding every cow and pig that grazed along the road belonging to the poor cottiers. It was whispered in circles, too, where his habits were best known, that his applications to the madeira and claret in his cellar were more frequent than appeared seemly for a preacher of the gospel— it was so quietly conducted, however, that, but for Mr. Thompson's confidential communications to the housekeeper, this weakness in such a shining pillar of the Church would never be known.

Some months passed away—his lady and sisters were on a visit to some friends in England, and were not expected home until Christmas.

In the month of November Lord Biggs went to a dinner-party at Colonel Dickson's, whose estate lay contiguous to Glengoulah.

As he was returning home, about an hour after

midnight, a shot was fired at him. He was riding in a small carriage, driven by the brave Jacob, so noted for his slender understandings.

The carriage had passed through the great gate, and his lordship, expressing a wish to alight, was assisted from it by the porter at the lodge, and he walked up the avenue. He had ascended the steps and knocked at the hall door, when he heard the report of the gun and saw a man running. He ran down the steps and tried to overtake the man, but fell in the attempt. On getting up he screamed for help, and then the door was opened and lights brought out, but the intended assassin was beyond their reach. A posse of police were sent for instanter, and while one portion were detailed to follow in the direction taken by the man who fired the shot, another portion, acting as a body-guard, accompanied his lordship to a magistrate to make depositions.

The bishop expressed a wish to make his charges to Mr. De Courcy, for malignant reasons of his own, and they accordingly proceeded to Cascade House. Mr. De Courcy and his household were all in bed, but the servants were soon aroused and showed the party into the library.

On learning their errand Mr. De Courcy came down in his dressing gown, and bowed coldly and formally to his lordship. The bishop addressed him immediately:

"Sir, one of your immaculate peasantry has attempted to murder me this night."

Mr. De Courcy unlocked his escritoire, seated himself, pen in hand, and, calling upon the constabulary present to act as witnesses, said to the bishop:

"You wish to make depositions, I presume."

"It was for that purpose I came here."

"Haley" (to one of the policemen), "please present that Bible to his lordship. You will please swear to the truth of the statement you are going to make."

"I can have no hesitation in doing so;" and he touched the book with his lips.

He then detailed the circumstances as just related.

"Do you think from the report was it a pistol, my lord, or a gun, which was fired at you?"

"It was a gun."

"You judge so from the report?"

"Not that alone; I saw the gun in the villain's hand."

"Oh, you saw him, then?"

"Yes; most distinctly. I saw his countenance fully, and looked at his profile. His face is indelibly fixed on my mind. There was no moon, but it was dusk, or darkish twilight."

"Do you know who he is?"

"No; the scoundrel is a stranger to me."

"Have you reason to suspect any one, my lord?"

"Yes, sir. You well know I have reason to suspect the whole vile crew of my tenantry, any one of whom would gladly take my life; but this wretch, I presume, is a stranger, whom they hired to murder me, being too cowardly to do it themselves. I have no doubt that it is a plot that has been long in contemplation."

Mr. De Courcy turned upon him a stern look. "My lord, you must confine yourself to facts. I cannot notice your comments. This is not the place for them. Has your lordship any further facts to relate?"

"No."

The deposition having been duly read over, witnessed, and signed, his lordship and guard took their departure.

As Mr. De Courcy sat at breakfast next morning with his family, he was surprised to see the bishop's carriage stopping at the door, and his lordship and guard alighting from it. He received them in the library as before.

"I have come, sir, to make a new statement," said Biggs.

Mr. De Courcy again opened his escritoire, and prepared to write.

"I was so confused last night from excitement," proceeded his lordship, "that I could not recollect who my intended murderer was; but when alone in the silence of my chamber since I recalled his features, and remembered him to be a man whom I ejected from my land some few years ago. He has been prowling about this neighborhood ever since, as a laborer. His name is Dempsey—Bryan Dempsey."

Mr. De Courcy fixed a scrutinizing look upon the bishop as he uttered these words, and demanded—

"My lord, have you been drinking strong liquors since I took your deposition?"

"Certainly not."

"Do you remember you swore point blank, in the presence of witnesses, that you had a perfect view of the man's face, that his countenance was indelibly fixed on your mind, and that he was a stranger to you?"

"Yes; but I recalled his features since."

"And you would now swear that what you swore a few hours ago was untrue?"

"I tell you I recollected his features since."

Mr. De Courcy closed his escritoire.

"My lord bishop, I must remind you I am a magistrate, and not accustomed to allow any man to treat me with indignity."

"Then you refuse to take my deposition?"

"Most decidedly. You must go elsewhere with your trifling; it will receive no toleration from me."

He departed, foaming with rage, and betook himself to Margin, in whom he found a willing tool.

CHAPTER XXI.

It was two o'clock in the cottage of Bryan Dempsey. He and Winnie, with their three youngest children, had just sat down to dinner—the two older ones were at school in Tinmanogue with Mr. Rafferty.

One little girl of four years sat beside her father, who peeled her potatoes and divided his attentions between her and a blooming little fellow of two years, who sat opposite, beside his mother. Winnie held the baby—a fine infant of five months—on her lap, and fed it and herself together.

Winnie still looked very young and pretty, and was always neat and tidy in her person and house. Their little cottage contained but two rooms. The inner one, which you caught a glimpse of through the half-open door, contained a good old-fashioned bed, with curtains of dark chintz and fringed pillow-slip. Beside it was a kneeling-chair, or Prie Dieu, of painted wood. Those were the gifts of her mother to Winnie on her marriage.

Over this chair, suspended on the wall, hung

several little framed pictures around a large-sized one of the Crucifixion, which formed a centre-piece. Our Blessed Lady repairing a child's garment, St. Joseph planing a board, and the Divine Infant between both, crumbling with his tiny fingers a piece of bread among a group of little chickens, formed the subject of one of the small pictures—rudely executed, but exquisitely touching in design. Another was the infant St. John carrying a lamb bigger than himself. A third was St. Patrick, dressed in full pontificals, standing in a commanding attitude with his finger pointing to the ocean, while a whole crowd of snakes, toads, and serpents, bounded or crawled as quickly as they could into the foaming waves, apparently very glad to escape from his formidable-looking crozier. A fourth was St. Bridget, wrapt in meditation before her inextinguishable fire in the "Holy Fane of Kildare."

A font of white delf hung close to the bed's head containing holy water, and a rosary hanging upon it completed the spiritual ornaments. The remainder of the furniture was humble but comfortable.

In the outer room or kitchen the ample fire-place had its usual pile of blazing turf.

Before this fire Bryan and Winnie were now eating their mid-day meal, as it is called, though it was two o'clock, the hour when all the laboring people take their dinner.

Opposite the front door of the cottage was another door leading to the little garden and potatoe-patch. A short partition protruded a little from this door, which hid from observation a settle bed that came down at night and accommodated the little boys with a sleeping apartment, and folded up in the day under a curtain effectually concealing it. The whole wall at this side was covered by a dresser, the pride of Winnie's heart, and the admiration of all who saw it. Here burnished tin, copper, delft, and china, contended for mastery. Each shelf was a study, and the *coup d'oeil* a mass of brilliancy perfectly dazzling to look upon.

In a nook near by was an alarm clock, which kept time to perfection, and two shelves containing their limited library.

A table white as snow stood under the window, and chairs white as the table were disposed around the apartment.

Over the fire-place was a portrait of a burly looking gentleman with a massive head, good humored face, and twinkling eye, dressed in a coat of bright green—while a scroll in his hand labeled " Repeal" told plainly as possible that it was the portrait of the renowned Daniel O'Connell, Esq., M. P. Beside this picture was another of a lady dressed in the height of fashion sitting before a looking-glass, giving, as we may suppose, the last finishing touch to her complexion, when she discovers, reflected in the looking-glass, the figure of a great gaunt skeleton close beside her, leaning on a scythe of very extensive dimensions. Without further ceremony he informs her she has to go with him, while she, not at all relishing the invitation, remonstrates in most moving language, to which he replies in terms more convincing than entertaining. The dialogue being printed underneath was a source of great edification to Bryan's visitors, who considered it a neat and instructive composition.

The outside of the cottage was literally covered with woodbine and Siberian honeysuckles, wherein Winnie displayed her early taste; and among the vines hung three cages, containing a lark, a goldfinch, and a thrush, whose combined voices kept the neighborhood in melodious strains "from early morn till set of sun."

Winnie herself often helped the feathered songsters.

When washing or scouring off her tables and

chairs she would rattle off "The Rakes of Kildare," "Kitty's Rambles," or some other equally lively air; or she would sing for the baby as a lullaby that beautiful old melody, "I'm asleep and don't awaken me," till the birds sat thoughtfully on their perches and listened. It was a pleasant little home, though not a rich one, for peace and virtue dwelt beneath its roof.

"Ah, then, Bryan," said Winnie, "did you think of asking Mrs. Keigan how she felt the rheumatics this year?"

"'Deed, then, it never once crost my mind."

"Oh, shame on you, Bryan; and you two nights under the same roof with her! How in the world did you forget it?"

"Well, I didn't hear her complainin'; and then, I didn't think of it. Anyway she was as spry as any of us, around the fire every night, singin' songs and tellin' ghost stories—we did not go to bed era night till past ten o'clock."

"Is that the work you were at? Indeed I heard some of John Keigan's ghost adventures before now and laughed till I cried again—he's the devil all out, at invention. Did he tell you about the night himself and Pat Rourke met the big buck goat down by Kitturnen church-yard?"

"Did he? Ha, ha, ha, ha! Sure I thought my sides would split. Pershume to you, for one John— every time I think of it I have to go off. Ha, ha, ha, ha! The laugh was contagious, for Winnie threw back her head in a kink, while the baby kicked and crowed, and the other little ones laughed uproariously.

Winnie wiped her eyes in her apron and was just resuming her dinner when a shadow crossed the open door and a constable entered the cottage.

Alas for poor Winnie and her little ones! That shadow was the most woeful that ever fell upon their lives. Long did the memory of that heartfelt laugh of poor Bryan's ring through the pleasant cottage, now dark forevermore—that laugh, so indicative of a peaceful conscience, for truly does the poet sing:

> "I never heard a hearty laugh
> Come out a villain's throat."

At sight of the constable Winnie turned pale as death. She had never seen one, since their eviction from their farm, without an inward ejaculation; and now again the baneful shadow stood within their home and all strength left her.

Bryan, though he had as little love for the genus as Winnie, was too mindful of his hospitable duties, and possessed too much of that inborn refinement so remarkable in all Irishmen—from the humblest peasant in his cot to the lord in his palace—to appear embarrassed, nor did he feel so in reality, for his soul was guiltless.

"God save you, honest man!" he cried cheerfully; "wont you sit and take share of our meal? It is not much, but it's the best we have, and you're kindly welcome to it."

"Thank you, no! Does Bryan Dempsey live here?"

"Bedad he does, sure enough; that's my name, sir."

"You will have to come with me to Mr. Margin's office."

"Mr. Margin's office? I think there must be some mistake. I have no dealings with Mr. Margin, nor hadn't for years."

"Didn't you hear the news, Mr. Dempsey?"

"No, sir; I heard no news."

"The lord bishop of Glengoulah was shot at last night."

"Good God! was he though? And is he killed?"

"No. He had a narrow escape of death."

"Thank God! I'm glad the unlucky old sinner wasn't killed in his sins."

The constable eyed him narrowly.

"They think you know something about it, Dempsey."

"Me, sir? Oh, bedad; you're jokin' now in earnest. If he wasn't to die till I'd shoot him, he'd be a long-lived man; and don't they know who done it?"

"I can't tell yet; but I was ordered to bring you to Margin's office. If you feel you are innocent, you can't object to come with me."

"Oh, sorra an objection I have. I wasn't even at home since last Tuesday. I was eight miles from here at a cousin's of my own, diggin' their potatoes. I'm only in town since nine o'clock this mornin', God be praised!"

"Well, my good man, you can state all this on your examination; it is useless to tell me." It is evident the constable was prepossessed in favor of the man from his transparent honesty. Bryan arose and took his hat. Winnie had not uttered a word since the constable came in, but sat with lips apart and dilated eye-balls, catching every word that fell from him. Now, that she saw her loved husband about to depart with him, an undefined sense of harm to come took possession of her mind, and restored to her a momentary strength. She started wildly from her seat, hurriedly laid her baby in its cradle, and clasping him frantically in her arms, exclaimed: "Bryan! Bryan, asthore; machree! Don't go near them. Don't you know that villainous Biggs thirsts for my father's blood? and seein' him beyond his reach, he will murder him through you! Darlin' of my heart, he will never let you out of his clutches, and your poor Winnie will see you no more! Oh, God pity me! Bryan, don't go near them blood-hounds; they're on your track! I see it all before me; your innocence wont save you with them—they don't care for guilt or innocence; they want the poor man's blood, and little trouble they'll take to find out the truth so as they have the victim!"

"Winnie, my poor colleen!" said Bryan, tenderly. "Don't let your fears make you spake so foolish. Don't you know there's law in the land? and it's against common sense to think they can swear away my life, when I have plenty to prove I was eight miles from the place where they say the crime was committed! Nonsense, Winnie! have sense. I'll be home wid you to-night, or to-morrow at furthest, please God."

"Oh Bryan, my own true husband!" and Winnie wept convulsively on his breast. The children all commenced screaming as they saw their mother cry.

Poor Bryan went from one to another, embraced them hastily, and hurried away with the constable.

CHAPTER XXII.

Many of the neighbors had gathered in when they heard the cries and saw Bryan Dempsey in the company of a constable. Curses, heavy and deep, were unsparingly bestowed upon "Biggs, and the whole crew of murdherin' thieves." The shadow of a doubt of Bryan's innocence never crossed the mind of one individual; he had not an enemy on earth but the wretches in whose presence he was about to stand, nor did even they hate him personally; he was but a tool used for the maintenance of the sordid landed interest. When he arrived at Margin's a posse of policemen were waiting to convey him to the castle, in the hall of which were assembled some country people and several magistrates. Margin, taking Dempsey by the shoulder, placed him among about twenty country people, and then proceeded with the farce of an examination.

"Now, my lord, cast your eyes over yonder crowd and see if you can recognize your intended murderer."

"Yes; I see him there among the crowd. It is Bryan Dempsey. He is the man who knocked me down with a horse-pistol. I now recognize him fully; he repeated the blow five or six times. I struggled with him, and knocked him down once."

A warrant was issued immediately for the arrest and imprisonment of Bryan Dempsey in Ardmore jail. Before night people of wealth and position offered any amount of bail for the temporary release of Bryan until the day of trial, but no bail would be taken.

It would be vain to attempt describing the anguish of poor Winnie, although she was surrounded by that sympathizing charity so abundant in the Irish heart for those in misfortune. One of the neighbors had started off for her parents and soon she had her loved family about her, but their very presence seemed to make her miss him more. She would start every moment, thinking she heard his step, or the sound of his voice, and going to the door would strain her eyes wildly down the Ardmore road, and return moaning bitterly, exclaiming, "Oh, no! no! My heart's life, you'll never come that road again!" To reason with her was vain. She said her heart told her the face of Bryan Dempsey would never more be seen alive in their little home.

Father Esmond, now bent by age and infirmities, was confined to his bed by a severe attack of asthma. When he heard of the arrest of Bryan Dempsey for such a crime he immediately sent Father O'Tool to offer every consolation in his power to his afflicted children. He had known both from childhood, and well knew they would not injure the humblest of God's creatures. Perhaps, of all the tenantry evicted four years ago from the Glengoulah estates, the one who murmured least was poor Bryan—not that he suffered less than others, for he had an old grandmother who was over ninety years, and was bed-ridden for five years before; and he had a father who was stone blind, not to speak of his young wife and three children, to all of whom he was devotedly attached—but his nature was of that cheery, hopeful character which always looks at the bright side of the picture, and his song was ever of "the good time coming." Even now in his prison cell, though he chafed over it when alone, he ever spoke cheerfully to his friends, especially to Winnie, telling her pleasantly she was a little goose to be making a sprinkling-pot of her eyes, for he would be soon at home with her, rocking the cradle, and smoking in the chimney corner. He did really believe so himself; and how could he think otherwise?

He was arrested on the 19th of November, and remained in prison until the following January, when a special commission was appointed to try the case. For the benefit of those who are unacquainted with the customs relating to the trial of prisoners in Ireland, I may as well state that there are two general assizes held throughout the country—one in spring and one in summer—at each of which two judges preside, one to try civil and the other criminal cases. All minor offenders are disposed of at the quarter sessions held in each county town. If, however, the crime be of a very aggravated character, and the country in such a state of disturbance as to alarm the peaceably disposed, the loyal gentry convene a meeting and petition the chief governor, or lord lieutenant, as he is called, to order a special commission to be held, in order to strike terror into the evil doers. This is a very expensive proceeding, and, as the tax for its payment is levied off the county, it is always a very unpopular one, and only resorted to in cases of the most urgent necessity. The present case was deemed one of that nature. The person of a dignitary of the Church by law established had been murderously assailed, and the inviolability of the whole landlord class had been struck at through him. Such a state of things was not to be borne.

A great meeting of the landed interest was held at Ardmore, and a deputation sent to Dublin Castle, praying his excellency to appoint a special commission to try Byran Dempsey, as it was essential to strike terror into all evil disposed tenants. Accordingly the commission was appointed, to be opened on Tuesday, January 20th, 1846.*

The court opened at eleven o'clock A. M., when the chief justice of common pleas and the chief baron of the exchequer took their seats on the bench. The town was crowded from an early hour by people from all parts of the surrounding counties, who were most anxious about the result of the proceedings.

An immense number of constabulary were collected in the town, both horse and foot. Notwithstanding the declaration of the landlords that the country was plunged in agrarian outrages, the only case of any importance on the calendar was that of firing at the Right Reverend Bishop Biggs, of Glengoulah Castle.

A large number of Catholic clergy of the surrounding districts were present during the trial. The court was thronged from an early hour by the gentry of the county. A vast number—in fact all

---

* See the account of Bryan Seery's trial, January 20th, 1846 ("for an attempt to murder Sir Fras. Hopkins, Bart."), by special commission held at Mullingar, County Meath, Ireland.

the jurors of the county—were summoned, and a very full attendance of both grand and petit jurors was the result.

When the writ of commission was read by the clerk of the crown the long jury panel was called, and a number of gentlemen sworn in on the grand jury. The chief justice of common pleas then charged them. He said: "Gentlemen of the grand jury, I very much regret that the state of this county has been such for the last five months as to render it expedient for you to assemble at this unusual period, and within a few weeks of your being impanelled at the approaching assizes. On looking, however, at the official return of the outrages that have been perpetrated since the last assizes, I am not surprised that those who naturally feel the deepest interest in the welfare of this county should endeavor speedily to put an end to this state of things, and by a prompt administration of the law to overawe the disturbers of the public peace, and to afford security and protection to the unoffending and industrious, and to restore tranquillity and order. Gentlemen, it is not my intention to enlarge on the disastrous consequences which would result from permitting your county to remain any longer in the state in which it unhappily has been for some months past. I purposely and studiously abstain from doing so, because I am anxious to avoid adverting to any topic calculated to inflame or disturb that calmness with which it is so desirable that all who take part in the administration of the criminal law should approach the discharge of their solemn duties. Gentlemen, from the experience I have so frequently had of the manner in which you discharge your duties as grand jurors, I feel that you do not require any explanation or instruction from the court. I have the fullest reliance on the intelligence and intention with which you will proceed in the examination of the different charges which will be brought before you. You will not, I am satisfied, suffer any indignation at the outrages that have been committed, to excite a prejudice in your minds when you are weighing the evidence against each individual accused; and, however those who have been engaged in the offences which we deplore may have insulted and violated the laws, I hope we shall let them see that those laws will be administered on the present occasion not more for the detection and punishment of the guilty than for the protection and safety of the innocent, or even those with respect to whose guilt there can exist a rational doubt. With these few observations I shall dismiss you for the consideration of the business which is prepared to be laid before you."

The grand jury then retired. Bills were sent before them, and immediately " a true bill " was found against Dempsey for shooting at Bishop Biggs. Dempsey was then placed at the bar. The indictment contained twelve counts. After twenty challenges on the part of the prisoner a jury was sworn.

The clerk of the crown, having read over an abstract of the usual indictment, asked the usual question. The prisoner in a firm voice pleaded " not guilty." The long jury panel was then called over, and eighty-four gentlemen answered to their names. A jury was selected from them, four of whom were magistrates.

CHAPTER XXIII.

BRYAN DEMPSEY was indicted in the usual form: " For that he, on the 18th day of November, not having the fear of God before his eyes, aided by some person unknown, unlawfully and maliciously did cut and wound the Right Rev. Samuel Wilson Biggs, Lord Bishop of Glengoulah and Ardmore, with the intent to kill and murder him," etc. The attorney-general then arose and said: " It appeared to him to be a case where all the witnesses should be removed from the court."

Chief Baron—" Very well; let all the witnesses withdraw; if they remain they will be fined."

The witnesses accordingly retired.

The attorney-general proceeded to state the case. He said: " From the abstract of the indictment which they (the jury) had heard read, they would be able to understand the general nature of the offence with which the prisoner at the bar, Bryan Dempsey, stood charged before them. It was one of many cases which unfortunately had occurred in the county in a short period, and which disgraced it. From the nature and number of these offences it was deemed expedient to call the county together on this very extraordinary occasion, with a hope that by a prompt and effective administration of the law the progress of such crimes might be arrested. It was thought necessary to issue a special commission in order to investigate the case now before them—a case in which the evidence appeared to him to be of so clear and satisfactory a nature as to warrant an expectation that the perpetrators of the offence would be brought to speedy justice. The present case was of that class for most, and the crown did not call on the jury for a verdict unless the evidence was of that nature to render it clear. He was sure the jury would give the matter their fullest consideration, and unless the evidence for the crown was much shaken with regard to truth, they would find a verdict of guilty. Of course, if they had any reasonable doubt of the guilt of the prisoner, they would give it to him, and find a verdict of not guilty." He then proceeded to call the witnesses. The first witness called was the Lord Bishop Biggs, who was examined by Sergeant Poker.

"I live at Glengoulah Castle, in this county, four miles from Ardmore. I recollect the 18th of November last, and went out to dinner at 7 o'clock in a small carriage driven by an English servant. I dined at Colonel Dickson's, and left it at 25 minutes past 12 o'clock. I suppose there were about twenty persons at the party. I was perfectly sober. There was no moon, but it was dusk or darkish twilight. I got out of the carriage in the avenue, and walked up to the hall door. I then walked up the steps, rang the bell, and when turning around heard a shot and saw the smoke. I saw a man, who ran. I followed him, and in the distance of about thirty yards came up with him. There is a bank there, and I fell; the man fell also. I got up, saw him with a gun, seized it, and then throttled him. I saw his countenance full, and looked at his profile. The man's face is indelibly imprinted on my mind. I took hold of him, looked over my shoulder, and saw a second man. I let go the first, and the second presented a pistol at me. He pulled the trigger, but fortunately it did not go off. I knocked him down with my left hand, and struggled with him. The second man knocked me down, and repeated the blow five or six times. The blow was with a horse-pistol. I cried out 'Help.' The hall door was opened; and when a light was brought, the man ran away. I saw the man the next day, and see him now in the dock—it is Dempsey. I know him for eight years. He was a tenant of mine, and was evicted about four years ago. He was a peaceable tenant. When I dispossessed him I promised to get him another farm and pay a year's rent for it. He never said he was dissatisfied. When I seized him he had no hat on—the hat he used to wear had a peculiar cut, and any one would know it. I saw it at Glengoulah next morning—it is the same he used to wear before. I saw a coat next morning—it was the prisoner's. I got five wounds in the head, and Dr. Ferguson attended me in an hour. I took means next morning to have the party arrested."

Court—" Did you communicate the name to any one ?"

Prisoner's counsel objected, but the court allowed the question to be put, and witness replied:

"I described the person, and in consequence the prisoner was arrested (identified the hat and coat). That is like the hat the prisoner always wore when I saw him."

Counsel—" You swore two informations next morning ?"

"Yes. Can't say I mentioned about the hat."

Counsel handed the witness one of the informations and told him to read it, which he did, and said: " There is nothing about a hat in this."

"Read the second information."

"There is nothing about a hat in this either. I swore the second information after I remembered it was Bryan Dempsey who had fired at me. I know him for years, and saw him the following afternoon, about five o'clock, at Glengoulah, when he was brought into the hall. There were several magistrates there, and several country people also. There was only one man among them that I recognized. They put Dempsey among the country people. Don't know what magistrate did that. Thomas Selling, my butler, gave me the hat. I don't know if he is in town at present. The sergeant of police showed me the coat. I think I saw it in his hands first *the following day at five o'clock*. The butler gave me the hat in the morning. I did not see the coat until five o'clock. Don't know what the sergeant has sworn to now, if he has sworn at all. I have heard that he did swear an information. I have no means of knowing the fact. I don't know if he is to be a witness here. I don't know if Constable Dougherty has sworn an information. I never heard his name before. Never heard there was a joint information sworn by the constables. Did not speak to the sergeant about the hat. Sergeant heard me say I knew the coat. Dempsey was my tenant, and surrendered his farm peaceably. We parted apparently good friends. I don't know where the coat is. It was twenty minutes to one when I came home on the night in question. I had no reason to complain of the prisoner's character or conduct while my tenant. If he had had capital, I would have continued him. I never heard any complaint against him."

Three servants of Lord Biggs were examined to prove the finding of the hat and coat near the scene of the attack. Two policemen and Sandy McGlauren swore positively the hat belonged to Dempsey.

Mr. Clements, Q. C., then addressed the jury on behalf of the prisoner. He dwelt much on the quiet, peaceable character given of him by the landlord himself, who declared he never appeared dissatisfied, nor grumbled at his being ejected, all which tended to prove he could have no motive for perpetrating the crime laid to his charge. He said the whole case rested on the evidence of identification given by his lordship, who had an opportunity of seeing the person only in the dark and dead hour of night, after coming from a party. The bishop swore an information next morning, but the name of the prisoner he never mentioned (he here read the information). Would they credit an humble peasant who would swear such an information? The prisoner was a tenant of the bishop, and did he in his information ever state that Dempsey was the man who fired at him? His lordship had made a mistake; and he (Mr. Clements) was prepared to prove it. With reference to the evidence given by the policeman, it was painful to witness the exhibition made there that day. If human lives were to depend on such evidence as that given by them no man in society would be safe. They never had the hat in their hands and only saw it once, but when or where they could not tell; and yet the jury were called on to take away the life of the prisoner at the bar on the proof of identity of a peasant's hat! God forbid people's lives should depend on such evidence, or that a jury could be found to convict a man of capital felony on such swearing! It was even six days after the prisoner was arrested that the informations were sworn by the policemen and land-steward about the hat. He would ask them, as honest, conscientious men, could they find a verdict against the prisoner. He would now proceed to give proofs which would save the prisoner's life, without even the shadow of a doubt as to his guilt. He would account for the prisoner on that night by persons of respectability, and beyond doubt. The evidence that would be given was, that the prisoner, after leaving his farm, took potato ground from his uncle, a man named Keigan, and a most respectable farmer. On the Monday before the outrage the prisoner went to dig his potatoes, and was asleep eight miles away from Glengoulah at the time the bishop was attacked. He would now prove his case.

Bridget Keigan swore that on the night of the attack Dempsey slept at her house. She saw him at ten o'clock on the Monday night, and after locking the doors went to bed. On getting up next morning she found them still locked as she left them. The prisoner came down stairs with her son some time after. He slept there on Tuesday night also. Glengoulah is eight miles from where Mrs. Keigan lives. Mary and Catharine Keigan, daughters of the last witness, corroborated her statement in every particular.

John Keigan examined: Remembers the time Bishop Biggs was fired at, and when the prisoner was arrested. Gave the same account of the transactions mentioned by the other witnesses. He said the prisoner slept with him on Monday night and on Tuesday night. The witness got up on Tuesday morning at daylight, and the prisoner got up also.

Mr. Gordon—"On your oath, from the time you went to bed on Monday night, until you got up, did Bryan Dempsey leave the room?"

"He did not leave the room that night, nor could not without my knowing it. I was never at Glengoulah Castle, but I know where it is. It is eight miles from my father's; and a person going there must either go that distance, or fly across the lake."

Some other witnesses were examined, but their evidence was totally void of public interest.*

---

* This account of the trial is taken verbatim from the Dublin *Nation* newspaper of January, 1846, and February.

CHAPTER XXIV.

The Reverend Father Esmond, though gasping with asthma, and leaning for support upon the arm of Mr. De Courcy, arose and gave a very high character to the prisoner, having known him from childhood. He said: "His filial piety to a blind father and a paralyzed grandmother were the admiration of all who knew him. When a mere stripling he was deprived by death of a mother's care, and yet he seemed to cling with all the more tenderness, and a gentleness almost feminine, to the infirm beings whom Heaven had left dependent on his youthful care. For many years he was seen, by hundreds now listening, every Sunday at the chapel of Tinmanogue, lifting his helpless parents from the car in which he brought them, and tenderly supporting them to the seat provided for them near the altar. This attention he never slackened, even when he became a husband and a father, or when evicted from his farm and placed in altered circumstances —never until he laid them respectfully to rest among their kindred dead. I have watched him too in

the relation of husband, father, neighbor, friend—
in all he has been the true man; upright, honest,
brave, high-principled. At the time when he was
evicted from his farm, when the fire was quenched
from his hearth, and his helpless parents carried out
in torrents of rain, almost on the eve of Christmas—
I was an eye-witness of it all—the only tongue that
uttered no unkind word was that of Bryan Dempsey. He actually endeavored to turn their misfortunes into a subject of merriment, trying to infuse a
spirit of cheerfulness and hope into the hearts he
loved—a spirit which I well knew he did not himself feel; but Bryan Dempsey was a stranger to self—
he lived only in those he loved. Had I a hundred
lives, I would stake all this moment on the innocence of Bryan Dempsey. He never lifted a hand
to injure any man; nay, I verily believe he never
harbored an injurious thought of his greatest enemy.
This virtuous man, gentlemen, is a very humble one
in the eyes of the world, but very dear to the heart
of his Heavenly Father. See you touch not a hair
of his head!" The venerable old man became so excited during his brief speech that his eyes flashed
and his face glowed, while tears streamed down his
aged cheeks. At the conclusion of his speech sobs
and cries attested the deep feeling which touched

every heart. Even the very wretches who thirsted for the blood of this virtuous peasant remained silent for some time for very shame. The gallant prisoner, who bore himself so bravely all through, was so overcome by the noble testimony borne by his venerable friend and spiritual father that he leaned over the dock and sobbed like an infant. Mr. De Courcy then arose, remarking " that it would be superfluous to add another word to the testimony of Father Esmond regarding the prisoner's character, in every sentence of which he concurred, having known Dempsey since he was a baby in his mother's arms." This closed the defence.

Sergeant Babbett then proceeded to reply on the part of the crown. His observations were confined to the evidence.

At nine o'clock the chief baron proceeded to sum up the evidence, which he did by reading the testimony given by the witnesses, and offering a few brief observations as he went along. The jury then retired.

At half-past ten they came out and said there was little probability of their agreeing, and asked for a fire and their coats.

Bailiffs were then sworn, and the court adjourned to eight o'clock in the morning.

Oh! what a night of anguish for that virtuous family—the alternate feelings of hope and despair which scorched their souls! None thought of sleep, and many of the neighbors came to watch with them. The chief baron said if the jury agreed before twelve o'clock he would come and receive the verdict. At eight o'clock on Wednesday morning his lordship sent to know if the jury had agreed, but was answered in the negative. It may be remarked here that the jury panel contained the names of *every gentleman who had signed the requisition for the issuing of this commission.*

At ten o'clock on Wednesday the chief justice of the common pleas and the chief baron took their seats on the bench, when the jury were called into court.

Chief Baron—"Well, gentlemen, have you agreed to your verdict?"

Foreman—"No, my lord; we have not."

"Is there any likelihood of your agreeing?"

"Not the least, my lord."

"Under these circumstances, gentlemen, you must again retire to your room. There is no alternative; we have no discretion in the matter."

"My lord, there is not the least use in our retiring again, as there is no possibility of our ever agreeing. There are ten of us one way, and two another; so, my lord, you may be good enough to discharge us, for agree we never will on this case. We are now twenty-four hours locked up in our room, with only some water for refreshment, and a very indifferent fire, and some of us in very poor health indeed. Our room is more like a dungeon than anything else. If we are confined any longer it may seriously endanger our lives."

"It is indeed a great hardship, gentlemen, and we feel very much for your situation; but we have not the power, gentlemen, under the circumstances, to act otherwise. You must again return to your room."

"My lord, if there was the most remote probability of our agreeing we would not make this application; besides, we are likely to be starved to death if we are kept any longer confined."

"It is a great hardship, no doubt, and I assure you we feel for your situation; but we can do nothing. You must again retire, gentlemen."

Chief Justice—" We feel conscious of the situation you are in, and feel very much for your position. Perhaps, if you look over your notes, you may come to some conclusion; and if you require any assistance, the learned chief baron who tried the case will render you every assistance."

After a short discussion the jury slowly retired, protesting they would be starved. The court ordered a good fire to be put in the jury-room, which being done the jury were again locked up.

At half-past eight o'clock P. M. the jury, not having agreed to a verdict, were discharged, after having been locked up thirty-six hours. The attorney-general immediately announced that he would again put the prisoner on his trial on the Thursday following. This announcement caused the utmost excitement throughout the town; and the friends of the prisoner, who were very numerous and respectable, and even the prisoner's counsel, were taken by surprise, as they did not anticipate (notwithstanding their declaration of readiness) a second trial of the prisoner at that commission.

It was quite clear from the time the jury retired, that they would not agree, and the announcement made by the foreman, that there were ten for conviction and two not, was canvassed very freely as a most extraordinary intimation, and most certainly influenced the prosecutors to bring on the trial again. They determined, no doubt, to mend their hand next time in the selection of a willing jury, and thus secure a conviction. The general impression was that the prisoner would have been held over until the

Spring Assizes, when the excitement then existing on the subject would have ceased; but it was no part of the landlord plan to let reflection take the place of passion: a landlord was fired at, and some one must suffer for such a daring crime—be he guilty or innocent it did not matter a pin's point. Assuredly no one could be so mad as to suppose the life of a peasant, however guiltless, could be compared to the atrocious *attempt* to take the life of Samuel W. Biggs, Lord Bishop of Glengoulah, with its castle and its broad acres! The counsel on both sides were in attendance at the sitting of the court. The building was thronged to excess, and the town was filled with country people to ascertain the result of poor Dempsey's trial. The prisoner's counsel applied for a postponement of the case to the Assizes, but were refused. The most barefaced anxiety was expressed for a conviction, and all prudence thrown aside, so much so that the prisoner's most earnest friends gave up all hope of justice. From the judges on the bench to the constables at the doors, all thirsted for the blood of this innocent man. The judge's charge, respecting the outrages so very frequent in the country, was not only magnified but misrepresented. On Thursday, January 31st, Bryan Dempsey was tried a second time. After hearing a repetition of the evidence adduced on the first trial, and deliberating from eight o'clock to midnight, a verdict of *guilty* was returned by a packed jury.

Those present in court that night will never forget the scene to their dying hour. Rain fell in torrents, but the packed streets bore testimony to the intense anxiety of the people. The silence of the grave fell upon all inside as the foreman, pale and with trembling tongue, uttered the foul falsehood. The very lights seemed to flicker and blink with shame when the chief baron arose and expressed his concurrence with the verdict of the jury. Then putting on his black cap and gloves he sentenced Bryan Dempsey to be hanged on a day hereafter to be named! The heroic prisoner received the sentence with the greatest self-possession and nerve. Bishop Biggs, arising hastily, grasped the arm of the Marquis of Eastfield, and entered into an earnest conversation with the judges. The bishop seemed terribly excited. Soon the crowd began to sway from side to side, and whispers were passed from one to another, a rush was made for the doors, and it required the strongest efforts of the police and military, who were there in great force, to keep anything like order. Large groups of people, with each an impromptu spokesman or two among them, were discussing some matter which seemed to cause conflicting feelings of hope and despair.

Soon the news spread like wildfire through the town that a man bearing the worst description of character—a successful evader of the law, and altogether a desperate ruffian—had been seen running from the judges to Mr. Margin's office, and from Margin's to the priest's, declaring before God that he was the man who fired at Bishop Biggs. He begged the judges, for the love of God, not to hang an innocent man, for that Dempsey had no hand or part in the act, nor did he ever belong to Captain Starlight's company.

When questioned why he allowed an innocent man to be tried for so foul a crime, he stated " he never dreamed for a moment that any jury could find Dempsey guilty, but if they caught *him* he would be sure to be condemned. He declared he would have finished the bishop (and was very sorry he did not) but that his lordship was so drunk when knocking at the hall door that he staggered from the knocker to the bell at the side of the door, and he, firing in the interval of the slip, the ball destined for his lordship's body lodged in the door. He entreated they would try him then, and said he was willing to die to save a just man—not in expiation of such an act as shooting at Biggs—*that* he considered was no crime, but a virtue to rid the world of such a double-dyed villain—a serpent that sucked the life-blood of the poor."

Will it be believed: the whole prosecuting crew—judges and landlords—affected to believe him crazy, and recommended he should be sent to the lunatic asylum and have his head shorn! Mr. De Courcy took this man's sworn depositions before two reliable witnesses. He then drew up the draft of a petition to the lord lieutenant, and lost not a moment in getting it numerously and most respectably signed. In fact every man of known worth and integrity was happy to sign such a memorial—even one of the jurors signed it. Of course the wretched bigots and persecuting landlords, with a few of those time-servers, plentiful in every country, who fancy it looks fashionable to be opposed to poor people, held aloof, or yet worse, declared against the innocent man. Be not surprised, dear reader! they were the Pontius Pilates of this little episode. Such exist in every state of society, and in every country under the sun. Alas! for human respect. The fear of being "cut" by some little upstart Cæsar of the day shuts their souls to every noble sentiment, and extinguishes every spark of principle, without which man is unworthy of the name!

CHAPTER XXV.

Soon those legal murderers heard of the petition and immediately took counsel together, and appointing a deputation started them to Dublin. The viceroy was already closeted with a deputation of a very different character. Some half dozen gentlemen of high character and position, and bearing historic names, came to seek the god-like prerogative of *mercy* at the hands of the representative of the sovereign. Among them was the " observed of all observers," the Rev. Father Esmond, now on the verge of one hundred years, emaciated and drooping, laboring to breathe, and so weak as to be sustained by the arms of Mr. De Conrcy and Sir Lawrence O'Donnell, of Park Castle. His snow-white hair flowed down his shoulders, and nothing could be more affecting than the noble appeal made by the venerable father on behalf of Bryan Dempsey. The fire of his eloquence seemed to arrest for the time the disease under which he labored. His language flowed with the force and rapidity of a mountain torrent, tearing to shreds the vile efforts resorted to for obtaining a conviction of guilt; the vindictive motives which impelled Bishop Biggs; the heart-rending scenes of the eviction; the wondrous patience of the people; the firm conviction in every mind of Dempsey's innocence, even before the real murderer had appeared. He then dwelt on the unblemished character, high principles and sterling worth of this poor peasant whose life hung upon the decision of his excellency, and who awaited his fate with the heroism of a martyr. He wound up by saying:

"My lord, I beseech you hear my words! The voice now sounding in your excellency's ear is as a voice from the grave. This is my last appeal to mortal ear; in a few days more I shall be numbered among the dead. Soothe the dying hours of an old man who has spent nearly a century on earth, and God's blessing will rest upon you forever!"

The viceroy listened to him with the deepest attention, never taking his eyes from the venerable form. It is said he was visibly affected by the appeal, but yet he gave no decisive answer, merely stating he would consider the petition and give an early reply. "I would beg to remind your excellency," exclaimed Mr. De Courcy, "there are but a few days left; the 13th is named for the execution."

The viceroy bowed, and the deputation left actuated by conflicting feelings. Some had strong hopes of a pardon; others hoped and feared alternately. Father Esmond alone felt sure of a refusal.

"Deceive not yourselves, my dear friends," said he; "he has to die; I feel it, and his old priest has to pass him through that ordeal. Well, my God; your will be done! I know it. I have that last effort to make for my poor child; and then, O Lord! let Thy servant depart in peace!" Shortly after the friends of justice had departed the landlord deputation were ushered into the presence of the viceroy, whose prejudices they worked upon for their own selfish ends, declaring they could not live in the country if Dempsey were pardoned.

"It is necessary," said they, "that an example should be made, in order to preserve the future tranquillity and loyalty of the country; for, if the agitators can now obtain a triumph, they will burst into open rebellion against her majesty and her liege subjects!" or, in other words, they said: "It is expedient that one should die for the people. If you miss this man you are no friend of Cæsar."

Could any language be more alike?

The viceroy promised an immediate investigation of the case and dismissed them.

On the next day Father Esmond received an official communication from his excellency's secretary, regretting he could not comply with the prayer of the petitioners regarding the pardon of the prisoner Dempsey.

All were more or less disappointed, excepting two —Father Esmond and Winnie.

Despair seized on poor Winnie from the moment her eye lighted on the constable as he stood in the doorway of her happy home, throwing a shadow across the cottage floor, and a deeper and more lasting one across her heart. Frequently adverting to that day, she would say to her father:

"Oh, father! I wish you saw us that day; we were so happy. He threw himself back in the chair, and we both laughed from our hearts out. It was our last on earth. The poor little ones all began laughing too, even to the baby, who kicked and crowed. That set her father in a kink; when it seemed as if the sun went out of a sudden. And, och! och! it did go out sure enough, and will never rise again for me. Oh, father! father! how can I live and think of my brave Bryan dyin' on a gallows? And how can I look my poor orphans in the face? Oh, God! have mercy on my soul!"

Her father looking at her, compassion and re

proach mingled in his gentle features, would exclaim: "Oh, Winnie, my lannah bawn! what's that you're sayin'? I know you did not think of yourself, or you would not talk as if it was any disgrace to die a martyr for Him who died as a criminal for us upon a tree. Don't you know well, Winnie, if Bryan was not the heart's blood of a good Catholic he need have no fears of judge or jury? Do you think if he was an Orangeman, or such a Catholic as could be brought over—like some we know—they would touch a hair of his head? No, child; he would be working his own farm still, and living in the house where he and his generations before him were born. But God forbid child of mine was ever the wife of an unprincipled man. I always loved Bryan Dempsey; and a proud man I am this night to think that they could neither buy him with their wealth nor terrify him with their threats. If they hang him he will die a martyr; but they may not be so bad as you think, after all, Winnie. Don't be givin' way to such black thoughts; God is good."

"Oh, father! don't try to raise my hopes; I know well he has no mercy to expect from *them*. I know he will die a true and brave martyr. Oh, God! forgive me for repinin'. Father O'Tool was telling me and Bryan yesterday in the jail how they used to hunt priests in the time of Queen Elizabeth; and how, when they'd catch them, they'd half hang them, then tear their hearts out and they still alive, and cut them up in quarters. It made my heart sick. Father! how can human beings be so cruel? Sure, that's worse than the brutes."

"Brutes, child! I wouldn't name them the same day with brutes. When human beings lose the grace of God they sink below the beasts of the field. Yes, indeed, Winnie, we must belong either to God or the devil; if God abandons us to our own passions, sure we're blacker than any devil. The cross of Chri t be about us!" and Winnie and her father crossed themselves reverently. The 13th was named for the execution. I will not harrow my readers by describing the parting scene between Winnie and the husband she so devotedly loved, and their five little children. Not a tear came from Winnie, for her grief was past tears. She fainted many times, and was at last carried away insensible, amidst the cries of her little ones, by her afflicted relatives. Father Esmond and Father O'Tool entered the cell soon after Winnie left, and found poor Bryan prostrate on the floor, little more than half alive. This was the evening of the 12th; and before the jail was closed for the night a declaration was drawn up and witnessed by these two reverend gentlemen, two magistrates of the county, the deputy overnor of the jail, and one of Dempsey's legal advisers. The following is a verbatim copy of the document:

"*County of Wicklow, to wit:*

"I, Bryan Dempsey, now a prisoner in Ardmore jail, and to be on to-morrow executed, do most solemnly and sincerely declare in the presence of that God before whom I must shortly appear for judgment, that I never fired at the Right Reverend Bishop Biggs, that I never committed any act tending to injure him in person or property, that I never was cognizant of or party to any conspiracy or plot to shoot or injure the said Right Reverend Bishop Biggs; and that I am not guilty, *directly* or *indirectly*, of the crime for which I am to be hanged.

"Witnessed on this 12th day of February, 1846, by the undersigned."

Here followed the signatures.

Father O'Tool remained all night in the cell of the martyr, praying with him when awake, and for him while he slept. At length the fatal morning dawned. When poor Bryan awoke from his last living sleep his heart died within him, and the room seemed to swim around. Wildly he thought of his loved home and its dear inmates, and his heart yearned to see them once again; but a mournful voice seemed to sound in his ears—" Never more, Bryan Dempsey! never more! To-day you die a felon's death for murder!" Stretching out his hands, he cried aloud, "Oh, God! it is only a frightful dream; it cannot be!"

Father O'Tool was beside him instantly. "My poor Bryan, have courage!"

"Oh! father dear. Oh! father asthore, machree! Sure I never hurted any man in my life; it can't be they will hang an innocent man!"

Father O'Tool silently presented him with the crucifix. He eagerly grasped it, and pressed to his lips the representation of the bleeding feet. Sinking upon his knees, he exclaimed: "Oh, blessed Jesus! you died on a felon tree for love of me; and why should I refuse to die for love of you? Forgive the murmurings of my weak heart, and give me strength that I may die with the fortitude becoming a Christian. Oh, merciful Lord! receive my soul into life everlasting."

Father Esmond arrived early and administered to him the Most Adorable Sacrament for the last time, as he had also done his first Communion. He prayed with him long and tenderly, and told him many anecdotes of the wonderful graces and lights bestowed by the Almighty upon those who are condemned to death unjustly. Soon as the clock struck twelve they recited the "Angelus" together, and then Father Esmond said: "Bryan, my child! your hour of glory is come!" He answered, in a firm voice: "I am ready. I follow Christ. I declare I am an innocent man!" He then moved after the governor of the prison to the fatal drop, answering, while Father O'Tool repeated the litany of Jesus: "Lord, have mercy on me! Christ, have mercy on me!" When he came in front of the jail, the pale, haggard face and mournful eyes of him so full of life, and once so gay, smote every heart, and a cry of anguish burst from the few spectators present. Bryan held the crucifix in his hand and exclaimed, in a clear deep voice, which fell upon the heart in tones not to be disbelieved or doubted: "I declare before my God, that I had neither act, hand, part, nor knowledge of the crime for which I am going to die here!"

The consummation had not yet come: the victim was kept waiting for his doom for an hour afterward. It was reported that Sir Gideon Chapman, the commander of the garrison, was expecting a reprieve by the *one o'clock* Dublin train for a man who was sentenced to die at twelve! These lying and cruel reports, however, did not move the people to a belief that the overseers of the tragedy were sincere; they only made them more despised. One man asked of another in the street if the prisoner had fainted, or was the execution postponed? "No," was the reply. "He is too strong in his innocence, and they want to keep him on and off for a while to see if he'll die like a dog."

Poor Father Esmond, gasping for breath and shivering in every limb that cold gloomy day, still stood with the prisoner's hand clasped in his.

"Oh! father, asthore! your reverence is killing yourself for me; and what are a thousand lives like mine to yours? Oh! father, honey! you're almost dead; won't you go to the fire and sit down?"

"No, my poor child; I thank you most kindly. But you surely do not want to part with your old spiritual father?"

"Part? Oh, would to God I could have you with me before the judgment-seat; you would plead for my poor soul to the God of mercies."

"No, Bryan; you will be alone there; but you will stand before your Heavenly Father, who loves you more than I could ever do. I too shall be there very, very soon after you; we shall not be parted long. I feel it here. In a few days we shall meet again, and then—then, Bryan, 'eye hath not seen, ear hath not heard, nor hath it entered into the heart of man to conceive the joys our Heavenly Father has waiting for us!'"—the eyes of the venerable saint were fixed on the sky. "Do you not already hear the rushing of the angelic hosts around the throne of our King and our God? Already the far-off strains of celestial harmony strike upon my ear!"

Bryan fell upon his knees. "Father, give me your last blessing and absolution. I would not exchange this death for the wealth and power of the whole world."

Father Esmond laid his hand upon his head, and ere the last words died upon his lips the officials came to conduct him to the fatal drop. Both priests warmly clasped his hands; and Father Esmond, raising aloft the crucifix, exclaimed—(as Abbe Edgeworth did, in similar words, to Louis XVI.)—"Martyred victim of tyranny! go and be tried before a just tribunal!"

The old man fainted and was borne away as the drop fell.

All this time not a sound could be heard in the streets, not a footstep broke the awful stillness; and, except the clergy in attendance, the law officials, the reporters, and the military, who in large force surrounded the prison and stopped up every approach to it, not a human eye was bent to see this *example* of the law's vindication. All business was suspended; nearly all the shops in Ardmore—Protestants as well as Catholics—were closed. Traders, who had come from Dublin to attend the butter and wool market, usually largely supplied on Fridays, were disappointed to find not a single pound offered for sale, and the market as deserted as a wilderness. Deep grief was in every home, and it seemed as if the destroying angel had passed over the town—its streets deserted, its look so vacant and death-like. Once in a while a neighbor would pass from one house to another, and in the clenched hands and teeth and passion-dark faces there were signs of a spirit which unjust sentences could not allay. For an hour or two anxious, peering faces and tearful eyes were thrust out watching in the direction of the jail.

About four o'clock, as the shades of evening were beginning to fall, about twenty men passed through the principal street in the direction of Bryan Dempsey's home. They kept as much as possible the military step and walked two deep in solemn silence. The four foremost bore on their shoulders a bier, on which was a handsome coffin of black velvet, with a silver cross and silver handles. This was provided by Mr. De Courcy. In it were laid the mortal remains of poor Bryan Dempsey. Loud were the wailings and deep the anguish when the mournful cavalcade reached the cottage. When it was set down and the lid raised, Winnie was brought by her father to look upon the body of her young husband. They first all knelt down and joined in prayer for the repose of his soul, and strength for the bereaved widow. She then approached, shuddering; but, to the astonishment of all present, her countenance brightened as she gazed upon him. He was dressed in the brown habit of the scapular, and on his breast, in letters formed of white satin ribbon, were the initials, I. H. S. His hands were clasped together, as if in prayer, and held a small wreath of palm-leaves—the emblem of martyrdom. The hair was brushed back off his forehead, which was white as alabaster, and the handsome, manly features were calm and fair as marble. Not a feature was distorted—a smile even seemed to linger on the lips. Winnie gazed long in mute admiration. She thought she had never seen anything so beautiful At length, in a low voice, she said: "Father, who did all this for him?"

"Two ladies, asthore—Mrs. De Courcy, and Miss Clara Menville, the young lady that you mind was so kind to Norah Cormac. May God bless them both for it!"

The young widow looked in her father's face and then at her dead husband two or three times; then, uttering a wild cry, she burst into tears. They were the first she had wept since Bryan's arrest. The pent-up fountains seemed closed to all her sorrows; but this touching tribute to his innocence and worth broke the spell, and tears like the rain fell upon the lifeless remains of him she loved so well —blessed tears, which relieved her overcharged heart of its burden of woe, and rejoiced her parents to see.

a bier, on which was a handsome coffin of black velvet, with a silver cross and silver handles. This was provided by Mr. De Courcy. In it were laid the mortal remains of poor Bryan Dempsey. Loud were the wailings and deep the anguish when the mournful cavalcade reached the cottage. When it was set down and the lid raised, Winnie was brought by her father to look upon the body of her young husband. They first all knelt down and joined in prayer for the repose of his soul, and strength for the bereaved widow. She then approached, shuddering; but, to the astonishment of all present, her countenance brightened as she gazed upon him. He was dressed in the brown habit of the scapular, and on his breast, in letters formed of white satin ribbon, were the initials, I. H. S. His hands were clasped together, as if in prayer, and held a small wreath of palm-leaves—the emblem of martyrdom. The hair was brushed back off his forehead, which was white as alabaster, and the handsome, manly features were ca'm an' fair as marble. Not a feature was distorted—a smile even seemed to linger on the lips. Winnie gazed long in mute admiration. She thought she had never seen anything so beautiful At length, in a low voice, she said: "Father, who did all this for him?"

"Two ladies, asthore—Mrs. De Courcy, and Miss Clara Menville, the young lady that you mind was so kind to Norah Cormac. May God bless them both for it!"

The young widow looked in her father's face and then at her dead husband two or three times; then, uttering a wild cry, she burst into tears. They were the first she had wept since Bryan's arrest. The pent-up fountains seemed closed to all her sorrows; but this touching tribute to his innocence and worth broke the spell, and tears like the rain fell upon the lifeless remains of him she loved so well —blessed tears, which relieved her overcharged heart of its burden of woe, and rejoiced her parents to see.

CHAPTER XXVI.

CLARA MENVILLE had received an account from the superioress of the convent of the progress of the trial. She besought Clara to write, and try to influence her uncle in causing the liberation of this just man, that his blood might not be at his door. Poor Clara was in anguish of mind. She knew a letter would be unavailing; but if she could only reach Glengoulah she would throw herself on her knees and kiss his feet, and wash them with her tears—but, oh! how was she to reach Ireland? Her father was spending the winter in Rome, and she and her sister were staying at Toppleton Hall, Cheshire, the seat of Viscount Toppleton, a nephew of her father, whose lady, though an excellent woman in her way, was a rigid upholder of all the proprieties observed by ladies of rank. Clara, though perfectly aware of her weak points, undauntedly flew to her and passionately begged permission to leave by that evening's steamer for Ireland. She rapidly portrayed the heart-rending scenes now passing in Wicklow, and urged the impossibility of delaying one night without losing her reason. Lady Toppleton was utterly horror-stricken at such a breach of etiquette, reminding her how his lordship was absent in Parliament, and no one there who could with propriety accompany her. She would have read her a homily on the importance of ladies of rank being always calm and unmoved, especially by the occurrences of common life; but Clara, whose thoughts were far away, abruptly asked if she could not travel with her nurse—a respectable, middle-aged matron, whom she devotedly loved, and who always had remained with her since the death of her mother. Lady Toppleton, struck dumb with amazement, stared at her as though she feared the contingency hinted at had already taken place, and that her senses were clean gone. She arose and rang the bell, ordering her carriage immediately.

"Miss Clara Menville, go to your room!" said she, with haughty dignity. "I am going to the parsonage to consult with Mr. Audley on this affair, and shall in all probability impart the result on my return."

Probably not, Lady Toppleton: *nous verrons!* When the carriage was out of sight Clara rang for her nurse, and telling her it was a matter of life and death for her to leave Toppleton Hall and reach the

Liverpool railway station within half an hour, she hastily got packed a few changes of clothing, ordered her pony phaeton to the door, into which she jumped with her nurse, driving herself, as was her custom, with her "tiger" behind. As Lady Toppleton drove up the avenue from the parsonage she met the boy bringing home the phaeton, and learned from him, to her unspeakable horror, that Miss Clara and Mrs. Bunse were on the road to Liverpool.

The impulsive Clara thought the train was going at an unusually slow pace, while the truth was it was flying at the rate of forty miles an hour, and was in agonies when it stopped in a town or village. She could neither eat nor sleep. Intent only upon one thought—the saving of a fellow-creature's life—she threw to the winds the cold barriers of etiquette and position. Arriving in Dublin late at night, she flew post-haste to Glengoulah Castle. Day was just breaking on the morning of February 13th as she ascended the castle steps. Here she met a bitter disappointment: her uncle, they told her, left the castle the night the sentence was passed on Bryan Dempsey, and was staying at the Club House, Sackville street, Dublin, and the execution was to take place at noon that day. Mrs. Biggs was in England. Poor Clara wept most passionately—she saw the hopelessness of achieving her object now. Pacing the floor and wringing her hands, she exclaimed wildly: "Too late! too late! My God! must he die?" Throwing her arms around her nurse, she wept bitterly on her bosom. Then, starting up, a thought seized her—she would go to Mr. De Courcy, and see if anything could be done. Requesting Mrs. Bunse to await her at the castle, she ordered a carriage and drove to Mr. De Courcy's. That excellent gentleman and his wife received their unexpected guest with a thousand welcomes. They made every exertion to console her, but Clara wept long and sadly—all her hopes were dashed to earth —all her plans frustrated.

Mr. De Courcy told her the utter impossibility of getting a reprieve, even had she arrived in time; explained to her how the real murderer, struck with remorse, had declared himself the guilty party, and was willing now to die in expiation of his crime, and to save this innocent man; how Father Esmond had gone to Dublin Castle and pleaded for the prisoner in the most moving eloquence before the viceroy himself—but all in vain! Her uncle had sworn point-blank that Dempsey was the man—he could not be mistaken—so Dempsey must die! Clara's tears again flowed bitterly. "Can I do nothing?"

she cried; "have I fled from my home like a criminal, to be of no use to any one?"

"No, my dear young lady," said Mrs. De Courcy; "you were not permitted by the Almighty to take a useless voyage. I doubt not you are destined to play a most useful part in this sad drama. If you cannot save the condemned, you can console his young widow and bring comfort to his orphan little ones. We can all take our share in such acts as these."

"Oh, yes; thank God!" said Clara, springing up. "I thank you heartily for the suggestion. Let us go and be doing at once, for I feel that my heart will burst if I cannot do something for this poor victim. Oh, uncle! uncle! God pardon you!"

Mr. De Courcy insisted upon her taking breakfast before leaving the house; so having swallowed a cup of tea both ladies drove to the Convent of Ardmore first. Clara, on account of her connection with Bishop Biggs, felt a delicacy in intruding herself upon Dempsey's family, and wished to be directed by the superioress how to act. The reverend mother was overjoyed to see her.

"Well, ladies," said she, when all were seated, "if ever an earnest prayer to God was quickly responded to, surely mine was this morning. I am in such trouble for my poor child Winnie, whom we educated here, that I have been trying to think of every plan to console her. Her mother was here yesterday to ask the prayers of the community for her; she has not shed a tear since her husband was arrested, and has had frequent fainting fits. I have great fears for her if his body is brought home to her disfigured, as I hear is common after strangulation; and I was just thinking of getting some charitable woman to arrange his features after death, and to dress his body in the habit of Our Blessed Lady. Now the difficulty is to get permission to do this from the authorities. I can get plenty of pious Christians to perform the task, but they are poor, and consequently would not be heeded. I then appealed to St. Joseph, earnestly begging through his intercession that I might be directed to some influential person who would procure this favor for my employés. I was coming out of the chapel after making my petition for the sixth or seventh time when the door-bell rang, and the moment I saw you both I knew my prayer was heard. God be praised for all His mercies!"

"Most certainly, reverend mother," replied Mrs. De Courcy. "We can, no doubt, easily obtain your request. Mr. De Courcy has already ordered a handsome coffin to be sent for him through the same motive."

"Oh, Heaven reward him; it is just like him."

"Reverend mother," said Clara, in a low voice, "have you yet appointed the persons to do this work?"

"No, Miss Menville; but I know two respectable women who, I am sure, will do it for the love of God."

Clara grasped her hand. "Oh, dear mother! please permit me to be one of the persons and you will confer a favor on me."

Mother Joseph started. "*You?* dear child! Oh, no, no; that would be too much to expect."

"Ah! Mother Joseph! you do not deem me worthy?"

The superioress could not speak; tears streamed down her cheeks; she clasped the youthful heroine of charity in her arms.

"Oh, my precious child! how rich in God's grace! But it would be too frightful a task for one so young."

"No, no, mother; please do not refuse me. I came a long journey to save the life of this martyr; but as I have been unable to effect my object, do not refuse me this great favor. Mother, if you do not think me wholly unworthy, reject me not, I beseech you."

"My dear young lady, who could resist charity like yours? I shall send a very pious and respectable woman to assist you."

Mrs. De Courcy was struck dumb with astonishment—admiration succeeded; and as the high born Clara proceeded to beg as a favor a task from which human nature recoiled, she sobbed audibly. She had never seen charity like this before. "My God!" she cried to herself, "if this be Catholicism, give me light to direct me, that I and all who are dear to me may embrace it." An impulse of God's holy love immediately filled her soul with a feeling entirely new. The world seemed naught to her, and she felt an unaccountable strength vibrate through every nerve. Something seemed to say for her (as she declares to this day she never could say it herself): "Mother, I will be that assistant; I will not be outdone in generosity by this noble young lady, who sets me such an heroic example!"

It was long before the tender heart of Mother Joseph could reply, so entirely was she overcome by her feelings.

"Oh, wondrous love of God!" she at length exclaimed; "what are you not able to effect!" Turning her tearful eyes on Mrs. De Courcy, she said: "It shall be as you say, dear lady; I would not for worlds deprive you of the merit of such an action. Sure I am, Mrs. De Courcy, our Blessed Lord will bestow on you also the greatest gift in the treasury of Heaven." She brought down the brown habit of Our Lady of Mount Carmel, and explained its meaning to Mrs. De Courcy, who had never seen one before. Miss Menville was familiar with them already, but begged permission to make a wreath of palm-leaves from the garden. They drove to the prison, and had an interview at the governor's house with the high sheriff. Mrs. De Courcy introduced Miss Menville, niece of Lord Biggs. The sheriff bowed profoundly; and when Clara made her request he immediately assented, and directed the governor to send word to the ladies the moment the prisoner's body was cut down, and to have it conveyed to a room in his own house, and everything prepared for their reception. The intermediate time was spent by Clara in the chapel of the convent praying for the soul of him who was about to appear before his Eternal Judge, and begging mercy and conversion for her unfortunate uncle.

The governor came himself to announce that the

execution was over. Poor Mrs. De Courcy's heart sank within her, and she turned deadly pale.

"Kneel a moment with me," said Clara.

She knelt and repeated with her three Hail Marys, "in honor of the tears our Blessed Mother shed when the adorable body of her Divine Son was placed in her arms, that she would procure strength for them to accomplish the task they had undertaken."

They arose much strengthened and drove rapidly to the prison. Clara knelt beside the body of poor Bryan Dempsey, which was laid upon the floor. She closed his eyes and arranged his features, while Mrs. De Courcy combed back his dark chestnut hair, and was surprised how little horror she experienced in performing offices she once imagined she never could fill. Poor Bryan had carefully washed and shaved himself that morning, preparing for the reception of the Most Holy Sacrament, and their task was thus rendered easy. The governor's wife sent her servants to assist the ladies, but they would suffer no one to touch the body only themselves until the coffin came, when they accepted the services of the undertaker's men to put it in its last receptacle. When this was accomplished, they remained to keep watch beside the body until Toney Byrne, his sons, son-in-law, and a few neighbors came to convey it home. Toney was quite surprised to see Mrs. De Courcy in such a place. She drew him aside and told him who the beautiful young lady was standing beside the coffin, and detailed the part she had acted, and its motive, carefully remaining silent on her own share in the transaction. She then brought him to look at Bryan's body. Toney Byrne could not utter a word; but kneeling in the midst of friends he prayed silently, while great drops poured down his cheeks. Clara, immediately divining who he was, drew back with instinctive delicacy until he had concluded. She then approached, and taking his hand said, " Are you not Mr. Byrne?"

"Yes, miss. May God's blessing light upon you. I'll never forget till my dying hour what you have done this day."

"My good friend, I was not alone; to Mrs. De Courcy you are more indebted than to me."

Toney raised his eyes to Heaven; and again the great tears rolled, but he could not speak. His friends now lifted the coffin, and the mournful cavalcade moved on.

CHAPTER XXVII.

Bryan Dempsey's body was waked from Friday evening until Sunday. Father O'Tool went there two or three times each day, and members of the Purgatorian and other religious societies kept relieving each other at stated intervals of the day and night, saying rosaries and litanies for his soul. None others were admitted excepting his immediate relatives and old neighbors.

On Sunday the funeral took place at three o'clock P. M. to the chapel yard of Tinmanogue, where all his kindred slept. The procession was immense, and was attended by many gentlemen of rank, who wished to mark their disapprobation of this legalized murder. The tolling of the old bell and the measured tread of the silent multitude recalled to many the beautiful lines of Davis :

> "Why rings the knell of the funeral bell
> From a hundred village shrines,
> Thro' broad Fingal where hasten all
> These long and ordered lines ?
> With tear and sigh they're passing by,
> The matron and the maid—
> Has a hero died—Is a nation's pride
> In that cold coffin laid ?

> With frown and curse behind the hearse,
> Dark men go tramping on—
> Has a tyrant died that they cannot hide
> Their wrath till the rites are done ?
> Ululee ! Ululee ! high on the wind,
> There's a home for the slave where no fetters can bind.
> Woe ! woe ! to his slayers,—comes wildly along
> With the tramping of feet and the funeral song.
>   And now more clear
>   It swells on the ear,
> Breathe low and listen—'tis solemn to hear ;
> Ululee ! Ululee ! wail for the dead.
> Green grow the grass of Fingal on his head,
> And spring flowers blossom ere elsewhere appearing ;
> And shamrocks grow thick on the martyr for Erin.
> Ululee ! Ululee ! soft fall the dew
> On the feet and the head of the martyred and true."

Winnie returned home to her now desolate cottage, where the light of her life had been forever quenched; but the fountain of her heart's grief flowed freely, and a soft and tender sorrow now reigned where a wild and burning agony so long dwelt. She and her family blessed God for the change. Soon, too, she was called on to minister to the wants of those she was bound to by the strongest ties of gratitude. It was the intention of Mrs. De Courcy and Miss Menville to visit Winnie before the interment of Bryan, but on reaching Cascade House that evening from the jail poor Clara was seized with a violent fever, and by midnight was delirious. The terrible excitement she had undergone, joined with loss of rest and fatigue, told fearfully on her tender frame. Her nurse came from the castle to wait upon her, but Mrs. De Courcy gave strict orders that no one should inform Toney Byrne or any of his family of Miss Menville's illness, therefore they remained in ignorance of the sad event until the day after Bryan's funeral. The instant Winnie heard the news she repaired to Cascade House, and kneeling beside the unconscious Clara poured forth tears and prayers for her recovery. She would willingly have taken the place of Mrs. Bunse, but that bustling lady would not suffer any hands to tend her darling but her own. Winnie or either of her parents were there many times every day, and soon had the pleasure of hearing that their young benefactress was pronounced out of danger.

A new and severer trial now awaited them. Winnie, on her return from Cascade House one evening during the week, received a message that Father Esmond wished to see her. She flew to her dear spiritual father, whom she found propped up in bed with pillows, and breathing more freely than he had done for years. He seemed calm and collected.

"Oh father, honey!" cried Winnie, leaning over beside his bed; "is it true what they tell me, that you are better?"

"Yes, my child; the great drag is gone from my chest, and I feel light and easy. My good God is unfortunate landlord, and all who were concerned in the legal murder of your husband!"

Winnie gazed on the sinking features of the dying saint. She seemed choking for a moment, and then said:

"Father, I would willingly do it; but how could I ask such a prayer with my lips unless my heart went with it? Oh! father, asthore! I cannot tell a lie. I don't wish them harm; but I can't bear to think of them, nor to mention their names. Sure, God who sees my heart would not hear such a prayer! Indeed, father, I can't help it!"

"Then, my child, you must earnestly pray tha God may remove such bad feelings from your heart. You may rest assured our Blessed Lady will obtain for you proper feelings of charity if you strive to overcome yourself and say what I tell you. God does not expect impossibilities. He knows how sorely your poor human nature has been tried; and if He sees you trying to conquer it, He will shower upon you most abundant gifts and graces. Winnie, I asked this same favor of your poor Bryan before he was led to execution. He never hesitated, but went on his knees and joined most fervently with me. I asked him if he would like you and his children to pray for the same object, and he said he would very much. Your good, pious father has ever set you this example of Christian charity; but, Winnie, I ask it not for the love of father, mother, or of your old pastor, nor even to comply with the last wish of your loving husband; no, Winnie, not for any or all of these must you do this—you must do it for the love of Him for whom all our actions should be done—for our dear Lord Jesus, who prayed for the wicked wretches who nailed Him to a cross."

Winnie bowed her head to the ground and sobbed convulsively for a few moments; then rising, she said:

"Father, I will faithfully do as you tell me, and teach my children to do the same, with God's blessing, while there's life in my body or speech in my tongue!"

Father Esmond held out his hand, now shaking with the death tremor. "God reward you, my dear child. I can now die in peace. May the blessing of the Father, Son, and Holy Ghost, descend upon you and yours, and remain with you forever."

His voice grew faint, and Winnie called in Mrs. Malone, who administered restoratives. Reports flew around that he was in his death agony, and all the neighbors flocked in. Approaching midnight his agony really commenced. Father O'Tool put the blessed candle in his hand and held it there. Several other priests from the neighboring parishes were present, one of whom recited the beautiful prayers for the departing. To the surprise of all he joined in the responses himself. When the prayers were concluded he opened his eyes and looked around the apartment. Seeing so many of his parishioners in tears, he said: "May God bless you all, my faithful, loving children. We will meet again in our heavenly kingdom. 'Oh! how lovely are thy tabernacles, O Lord of Hosts! My soul fainteth for the courts of the Lord.'" He seemed transported in an ecstasy. After a moment or two he cried out: "Jesus! Jesus! receive my soul," and, turning his head on the pillow, calmly expired. Silence reigned around until Father O'Tool, extinguishing the light, sank upon his knees, and exclaimed: "Eternal rest grant unto him, O Lord!" and he burst into tears. Then the sobs and lamentations of the bereaved parishioners were mournful to hear. Ah! those were sorrowful days in Tinmanogue. A funeral pall seemed to hang over the beautiful village. Every shop was closed, every bell tolled—that of the convent, the old elm-tree he loved so well, the school-house, where in days of yore he spent so many hours instructing the boys now grown to manhood, and too many, alas! eating the bread of exile in a foreign land. All tolled mournfully, and bore the sad intelligence through the echoing hills around. The father, friend, counsellor, consoler, peace-maker, and pastor, so idolized for more than half a century, was gone from them—just when they thought they needed him most, and could least spare him. But so they would have thought any time he might be called.

> "Sheep without a shepherd,
> When the snow shuts out the sky."

The cruciform chapel, embowered in shrubs, was crowded night and day until he was laid in the tomb. A continuous stream of people passed and re-passed in and out, with tear-washed cheeks and sad hearts. They were taking their last look of their beloved father as he lay in his coffin, dressed in his ecclesiastical robes, his white hair floating down his shoulders, and his saintly features smiling. They waked him thus before the altar where he had so often celebrated the divine mysteries, and where his fatherly tones and venerable appearance so many times recalled to them the Apostles of old. But the family that mourned him most was Toney Byrne's, for they felt he had shortened his precious life by the hardships he had undergone, first by trying to save the life of Bryan Dempsey, and then in consoling his last moments.

He was buried in the chapel-yard among his flock; and, according to his own request, no fence was put up between him and his loved parishioners. His grave was beside the chapel, and on the edge of the centre walk, that all might find him accessible in death, as he always was in life.

CHAPTER XXVIII.

On the same night, and at the same hour when the venerable pastor of Glengoulah was conducted by angels to the throne of the Eternal Father, whom he ever strove to serve, while his last sighs were embalmed by the tears and prayers of his loving people, quite a different scene was enacting in Dublin.

In a sumptuously furnished apartment of the Club House, Sackville street, a man lay moaning on a bed of down.* Four stalwart-looking men in their shirt-sleeves watched beside him. Their strength was frequently put to the test to keep the wretched sufferer from jumping out of the window, or dashing his head against the wall; they were then obliged to force him into the bed, or strap him in a large invalid chair. Sleep had been long a stranger to his wild and frenzied eyes, and at times his shrieks were appalling.

"I tell you the truth, Jim," said one of the watch-

---

* It is a well-established fact that Sir Francis Hopkins was obliged to be strapped to a bed (after the execution of Secry) at the Club House, Sackville street, and finally died a lunatic somewhere on the continent.

ers, wiping great drops of perspiration from his forehead with a blue cotton handkerchief; "if they had a paid me last Saturday you wouldn't see me here to-night. The pay is good, to be sure; but, be the great King William, it's earned hard."

"Well, I wouldn't care a pin's point," joined another, "about his leapin' and jumpin,' if he'd only hould his tongue; but, upon me life, he puts the heart across in me when he does be jabberin' to some one unseen!"

"Yes, indeed. And between ourselves, George, I think the divil has a heavy mortgage on his soul; and, upon my conscience, but he'll have pleasant company when this ould fella goes home to him."

"Well, the divil sweep the whole of yees; but yees got to be mighty fine Christians all at onst," chimed in the fourth—a big, rough Orangeman. "Aren' yees worthy follyers of King William, to be echoin' the sentiments of the Papish brood? What if he did send some of them on an arrand to the divil a little before their time? Its good enough for the likes of them!"

"Hould your tongue, Alick! and don't be makin' a jackass of yourself. I can drink the glorious and immortal memory as well as any of yees, and shout 'To hell with the Pope!' till my lungs are hoarse, on the 12th of July; but, when all is said and done, I can't feel any spite to my Papist neighbors—and sure I'd have a bad right—for I don't forget, Masther Alick, how fast you ran from my bedside the night the doctor said I had the cholera—nor all as one Tom Hanlon, my door-neighbor, if he is a Papist. I'll never forget it to him. When he heard my wife cryin' he come in and rubbed and stuped me till the sweat run down his face—savin' favor—and he staid there wid me the whole night, till the danger was passed and it was clear daylight; and then he worked all day long at his trade. He's a stone-mason, and one of the best livin' men I ever seen."

"I suppose there's some good ones among them like ourselves, Joe;" and George nodded in the direction of Alick, while he chuckled to himself.

"Hould your divils of tongues; here's the doctors!" cried Alick.

Two gentlemanly-looking men came into the room quietly.

"Well, my men, how is our noble patient this evening?"

"Couldn't be worse, sir. He's after exhausting himself talkin' and screechin'. He thinks he sees a man followin' him constantly. We had to take down all the pictures and mirrors; he a'most went into fits at sight of them. One time, when we were makin' the bed, he caught sight of himself in the lookin'-glass and run under the bed, where he squeezed himself flat like a pancake. Be the Boyne, but it's hard work, your honors, to attind him. Myself wouldn't take tin pounds a night if I knew what was afore me; but I wouldn't break my engagement, onst I made it, for five hundred pounds."

Joe and George made a face at one another at the back of the physicians when they heard Alick's honorable account of himself. One of the doctors held his pulse until two other physicians entered; then all went into consultation. The consequence was he was strapped to the bed, his head shaved, and a large blister applied to the poll, while bags of ice were kept to his temples. The doctors remained all night, relieving one another at stated intervals. By morning he seemed calm. About eight o'clock A. M. the Kingstown train brought his lady and suite, who arrived by the mail boat from London. The physicians, after consultation, deemed it best to bring her to him unannounced. She walked with a languid air to the bedside, and began to weep in an embroidered handkerchief. He fixed his eyes wildly upon her, and convulsive tremors shook his frame. He said, in a hissing whisper, "Are you his widow?"

The lady renewed her tears.

"I tell you I can do nothing for you. I tried to save him since I came here, but they kept me strapped down. I told the judge the day before I left the castle not to hang him, but he said it was too late. Curse the old fool for being always too late. Curse you too, and the whole Papist crew; and curse myself. G— d—— you! don't you hear me cursing myself; and why do you cry? I can't give him back to you if you were to cry till doomsday. I know he's dead. I saw him hanging there—on that wall. He leered at me and grinned as he was going off the drop."

"Oh, dear husband! do not speak so horribly!" said the weeping lady.

"I tell you, woman! your husband did grin at me; he did! And oh, God! how frightful he looked! I see him again! There he is! He is always leering and mocking me!"

The lady turned to leave the room. He shouted after her: "Come here, you woman! I want to make a bargain with you. I'll give you your choice of the best farm in Glengoulah if you will keep him from following me!"

The lady now thought she would try to soothe him. "Oh, my dear! you are laboring under a delusion. There is no one trying to follow you. No one can follow you."

He made violent efforts to disengage himself from his bands, and failing he glared upon her and shrieked out:

"Do you dare tell me I lie? You are a cursed fool, you low, contemptible creature, to doubt the word of a bishop. I tell you a huntsman with a yelping pack after his heels is not more surrounded than I am. My life has been most miserable for more than a year. I had wealth and honors, but no happiness. I drank to drown my miseries, but it would not do—it was then I suffered most. A curse, I say again, upon my obstinate tenantry. They wouldn't hear the true gospel from me; but would believe their d—d old priests. I swore to make them Protestants, or to have my revenge, and I had it! Ha, ha, ha! I'm glad I made them suffer! I had my revenge! But, G--d d—n them! they have theirs now. Sometimes they all come together, and set me nearly crazy with their abuse; sometimes they come alone, but in such rapid succession that they bewilder me. Last night that old villain Flannigan was here abusing me for pulling down his house; he accused me of leaving him homeless and childless, because his children were drowned at sea on their way to America. Then Fogarty walked in to curse me, because his old mother died a lunatic, because she lost the farm and was starving. Then in came thirty-seven that were evicted from the townland of Drismore shortly before Christmas, each telling a dismal tale of suffering, enough to drive any one mad but myself. Then the widow Ryan came in and abused me because the bailiffs carried out her two children in the rain, and both sick in scarlet fever, and they died next day (she says). I verily believe they died just to spite me— these papists are very vindictive. Then in came the widow Cormac, and blew a perfect hurricane from her nostrils. I felt the bed rock under me, and everything was blown about; the snow began to fall, and she pointed to a heap of it that had drifted into a pile, and there that wild maniac daughter of hers lay dead. They never let me get a wink of sleep, but stand leering and grinning at me when they are tired abusing. I do not heed them, however. I crouch down and keep very still until they are gone. Then I try to get away, and scream out for help, but no one cares to save me. I could bear any of them—yes, all of them together—better than this Bryan Dempsey. I know you are his widow, and I feel really sorry for you; but I can do nothing for you while he follows me, and keeps pointing to his throat and grinning so terribly. Mind I promise you, on my word of honor as a gentleman and a Christian bishop, if you will keep your husband away I will give you a beautiful farm, and never molest your children in their religion. Will you do this for me? Papists profess to be charitable and forgiving—I will see now."

The doctors whispered her to agree at once. "Of course I will do it for you," said the unhappy lady. And, hoping to humor him, she asked: "What would you think of taking a trip to England, my lord? They say spirits cannot cross water, so they cannot follow you over sea."

"I should like it very much, indeed; but you must accompany me, or your husband will not stay away."

"Oh, certainly; I shall go with you everywhere."

This assurance seemed to calm him, and he was permitted to sit in his easy-chair; but he would by no means suffer her to leave the room a moment. He evidently took her to be poor Winnie Dempsey, and imagined he was freed from the ghastly vision of Bryan's death while she was present. In about a week the doctors pronounced him fit to travel, and they left for London.

As Miss Menville was lying in fever at the residence of Mr. De Courcy while these scenes were transpiring, she was not aware of the arrival of her aunt in Ireland. Mrs. Biggs, however, was duly waited upon by the housekeeper of Glengoulah Castle, and, learning that her niece was a guest at Cascade House, deemed it beneath her dignity to pretend being aware of that circumstance; she therefore sent her no message, and left before she had recovered.

When Lord Biggs and suite arrived in England they resided for a time in a fine mansion outside Greenwich, removed from all company or any excitement. The grounds were extensive and tastefully laid out, the landscape around highly cultivated, and every object inviting to repose. Here the bishop's health greatly improved, his paroxysms became less frequent, and hopes were beginning to be entertained of his recovery, when a circumstance occurred which rendered those hopes fallacious.

A large number of ejectment cases had been laid over from the last quarter sessions, in consequence of the landlord's illness, and Mr. Margin was at a loss to know how to proceed. Hearing that his lordship was rapidly recovering he wrote him for instructions several times; but receiving no reply he pondered over the case and finally came to the determination of paying a visit to the invalid. He thought, too, that this act of courtesy would secure him future favors; so off he started in the month of May for London, with a bustling and important air, sending his bailiffs around before his departure to warn the unhappy tenantry to be prepared for the worst on his return. Fresh consternation and renewed tears were the result of those warnings.

One lovely afternoon Lord Biggs was reclining in a large arm-chair on the lawn, enjoying the beauty of the evening and the charming landscape. He had a portfolio of handsome engravings lying before him on a rustic table. His valet had just gone into the house for a few moments, when a turn in the avenue brought a new comer in sight. At first he seemed not to recognize the person, but a few rapid strides brought Margin, bowing and scraping, face to face with his lordship. The unhappy bishop trembled like an autumnal leaf at the presence of the unwelcome visitor; but when the agent, making another profound obeisance, inquired after his lordship's health, maniac lightning seemed to flash from the bishop's eyes—he uttered a fierce growl and clutched Margin by the throat. Having, as before intimated, a diseased leg, and being taken unawares, Margin lost his balance and fell to the ground. The frantic Biggs jumped upon him and endeavored to strangle him. Margin screamed for his life, and the whole household rushing out he was saved from immediate death. But Lord Biggs's delirium returned in the most aggravated form. Mrs. Biggs bitterly upbraided Margin for presuming to speak to his lordship on business. He assured her he had not done so, and was merely commencing to inquire after his health when he fell upon him.

"No wonder he should," she replied. "It was your bad counsels and worse acts that made him unpopular with his tenantry, and made them reject the Book of Life and the liberal education offered to them and to their children."

"Is this, then, madam, the reward I receive for making the Glengoulah estates four times as valuable as they were under the agency of De Courcy?"

"Oh, don't you speak of Mr. De Courcy. Whatever his faults were, he was at least a gentleman."

"Madam, you evidently do not understand the case; permit me to explain—"

"Sir, I understand one thing—that your business is with his lordship's lawyers, Messrs. Hawse & Jones, of whose address you are well advised. You certainly have none in this house, and I beg you will withdraw."

Choking with rage and mortification, Margin for the first time realized the truth of the proverb:

"As you sow, so shall you reap."

He returned to Glengoulah much more speedily than he had anticipated; and if not a better he was decidedly a much more ragged man; for his new coat, purchased expressly for the occasion, was torn to shreds in the scuffle with Biggs. He was observed to be very taciturn and crest-fallen after his return. The ejectment cases were again held over until next session, and the poor tenants, for a time at least, felt secure of a roof.

The bishop became so untractable that he could not for a moment be left alone, as he attempted self-destruction several times. The doctors again recommended change of air and scene; so Mrs. Biggs, with their own physician, keepers from a lunatic asylum, servants, etc., left for Paris early in June and thence to different cities, crossing into Belgium, thence to Germany, sailing up the Rhine, and visiting every place of interest. All was in vain. Biggs seemed to become more frantic every new place he arrived at. His lunacy, however, took different phases. Sometimes he would shake with terror and hide away in holes and corners from the victims of his avarice. Again he would imagine himself in the plenitude of his power ordering their arrest, and swearing to wipe out the whole Papist brood, and colonize his estate with Protestants. Through all his language was a mixture of blasphemy and Pharisaical cant. He would curse priests and people; but his heaviest maledictions were reserved for Margin, whom he cursed in all moods, and vowed to exterminate root and branch, as soon as he returned. Finding change of scene ineffectual, they came back to England about the end of August.

A final consultation being held by the doctors, they recommended that he should be placed under the discipline of a private lunatic asylum immediately. This advice was forthwith acted upon, and the result was it terminated his madness and his life before the end of the following month. In the last week of September, just as the rent-day came on, strapped to an iron bedstead in a mad house, the unhappy sinner died! His last words were a malediction on Margin.

How inscrutible are the ways of Providence! How just His retributions! This was the end of all for *him* the fame of whose cruelties rang through all Europe!

The Right Reverend Samuel W. Biggs, Lord

Bishop of Glengoulah and Ardmore—the stroke of whose pen sent hundreds of virtuous people to the crowded towns to perish of want, to the emigrant ship, and to the grave!—there he lies dead in the cell of a mad-house, chained like a dog to an iron bed! Dead! without one friendly voice to soothe his last moments! Dead! without kith or kin to close his eyes, or a Christian tongue to utter one prayer for mercy on that passing soul so heavily laden!

"Sic transit gloria mundi!"

CHAPTER XXIX.

One clear, balmy morning in October, in that season which is poetically called in Ireland "The poor man's harvest," a woman of prepossessing and still youthful appearance, dressed in an humble garb of black, and holding by the hand a little girl with fair, clustering curls, was sitting in the parlor of the Presentation Convent of Ardmore. Soon a beautiful young lady entered, attired in the dress of a postulant of that order. Her soft, hazel eyes were lit up with a smile of pleasure as she caught sight of the widow, who immediately arose and courtesied. The young postulant exclaimed: "My dear Winnie, I am so glad to see you! and this is your little Mary?" She took Winnie's toil-worn fingers between her soft, white hands as she spoke, and then patted the child's golden curls.

"You were so good, miss, as to invite me to come to see you! And some of the neighbors told me you would be soon going to England again, so I took the liberty of asking for you."

"Winnie," said the young lady, earnestly, "have you heard the news from England?"

"Yes, miss; I heard it. God pity us all! Indeed, indeed, Miss Clara, I felt heart sorry for you!" Poor Clara covered her face with her hands, and Winnie wept in sympathy.

"Ah, Winnie, what a contrast! Which of them was the richer man? You have every reason to believe your dear husband is in heaven with God and his saints forevermore; but my wretched, wretched uncle died in his sins!"

"Oh, Miss Clara, dear! don't grieve your noble heart for one so unworthy. Sure, if he took your advice, or any one's with a conscience, it's alive and happy he'd be to-day. And they say many's the warnin' he got to let the poor alone, but he wouldn't heed them, and their cries pierced the heavens at last. My heart aches to see an angel like you shedding a tear for him!"

"It is because of his life of crime, Winnie, that I cannot help weeping for his miserable death. Remember, Winnie, his soul was created to God's image. Oh, what a disfigured image he made of it!"

"That's just the way my father feels when he speaks of his death. He mourns for his soul as if all belongin' to him was laid low. Sure, I know it's the right feelin', and I ought to think of these things too; but oh, Miss Clara, dear! pray God to forgive me. I can't for my life think of him but I think of my peaceable, happy home, if it was poor; and of the hearty laugh my poor darlin' was givin' when the peeler darkened our door! Oh! vo, vo, vo! A laugh will never be heard there more! Oh, Miss, honey! why did he choose out the purest and best man that ever lived, and persecute him to the gallows?"

Winnie was in one of her paroxysms of grief at the recollection of her devoted husband. She wrung her hands and raised her eyes to heaven in the abandonment of sorrow. Clara was awed into silence at this outbreak, so natural and so touching. She had never before seen such a manifestation of woe, and it added another link to the chain of evidence every day growing stronger on her mind that the Irish were a people of the deepest feelings. She did not dare interrupt a sorrow so sacred. After a while Winnie came over to ask her pardon. She said her heart was overcharged, and she could not control herself.

"Indeed, my poor child!" she said, taking the widow's hands in both her own, "I am very far from condemning your feelings; but, Winnie, I have not told you the news about myself. I have become an inmate of this convent; yes, indeed." And she smiled at Winnie's blank look of amazement.

"I am going to be a nun, please God. And do you know the favor Mother Prioress has granted me? I am to be called, in religion, Sister Norah. I wish to bear while I live the name of that dear child who first brought the dawn of faith to my darkened soul."

"And you are not going back to England, miss? And you are, for sure, going to stay with us here in Ardmore!"

"For sure and certain, Winnie. I wrote to papa for permission—he is in Rome; and from the favorable answer I received I have very strong hopes, through God's mercy, that he too will soon be received into the Church. He is about being converted. Now is not this delightful news? See how sweetly our Heavenly Father dispenses to us joys and sorrows, both alike to draw us to himself. And now, when your little Mary is old enough to come to school, Sister Norah will be her teacher; meantime you must all pray to the Blessed Mother to obtain for me the grace of perseverance."

Winnie felt happier that day than she had done since Bryan's death. She hastened home to communicate the joyful intelligence to her parents, and great were the rejoicings all through Glengoulah, Tinmanogue and Ardmore when it was known that the beautiful young English lady had become a nun.

A few days later it was announced that the Glengoulah estates had become the property of George Bentley, Esq., the nearest heir-at-law to the departed bishop. He was a country gentleman in England, having much property there, and being an excellent landlord he felt ashamed of the unenviable notoriety acquired by his predecessor, and was determined to leave nothing undone to repair the scandals now the topic of general conversation. He betook himself to Glengoulah Castle as soon as possible, and set about seeking testimony from both sides as to the character of the tenantry, the treatment to which they were subjected by both agents, the relative condition of the estates under the past and present regime, etc., etc. His cousin, Clara Menville, now Sister Norah, of the Presentation convent, gave him valuable aid in his inquiries. He visited the farms himself, and conversed with many of the tenantry—sent for some of the dispossessed, and promised to reinstate them if their conduct bore the investigation he designed making. Margin was the first to pay court to the new landlord. Mr. Bentley received him courteously, for he resolved to be perfectly unbiased in his judgment, and invited all, agent and tenant alike, to lay their grievances before him. Margin did not much relish this state of things, but he determined to have the first statement, and thus try to create a favorable impression of himself in the mind of Mr. Bentley. Accordingly he drew a frightful picture of insubordination, bigotry, lawless violence, arising from treating with too much kindness a people who were unable to appreciate it, always requiring a strong hand over them, or they would be sure to end in arson, or, probably, assassination.

Mr. Bentley listened attentively, made copious notes, but uttered no word of comment. Margin had strong hopes he would mar the evidence of his opponents by this timely eloquence, and corroborated all his statements by a written document signed by those political fanatics who made themselves so conspicuous on the trial of Bryan Dempsey, and by the honorable and truthful Sandy McGlauren.

Unluckily for Mr. Margin, about this juncture Lord Wallingford returned from a lengthened sojourn on the continent to the great delight of his tenantry, who strewed the roads with green boughs, and would have taken the horses from his carriage and drawn him home as in a triumphal car, but he would not allow it. Arcades of flowers were formed in every village through which he passed, even in those places where the people had not the good fortune to own him for a landlord. Such was the admiration and respect felt for a good man, who was always actuated by a sense of justice. About a week after this arrival a card, announcing a visit from Lord Wallingford, was handed to Mr. Bentley at the castle. They met in the library, and his lordship greeted Mr. Bentley most cordially and welcomed him to the county. After some general conversation, Lord Wallingford said: "You have a splendid property here, Mr. Bentley."

"Yes; but I was half afraid to take possession of it. I do assure your lordship, it required no small amount of both moral and physical courage to face the terrible dangers predicted for me by my friends in England, maiming for life being among the smallest. I take credit to myself for being a most valiant knight, and doubt not, if I lived in the ages of chivalry, I should have won my golden spurs while yet a stripling."

"Your danger or safety, Mr. Bentley, depends entirely on yourself. I speak to you candidly, as one man of honor should to another. You have come to reside among a people of deep passions and warm affections—a people keenly alive to a sense of wrong, but so long loaded down with oppression as to receive as favors and repay with sincerest gratitude those common acts of justice which you are every day accustomed to render to your English tenantry, and which they expect *as a right*. You will find plenty to convey to you a very different character of this people, but if you are the man of sense and honor I take you to be you will not allow your judgment to be warped."

"But you forget, my lord, that I am a stranger. How am I to judge, except by the testimony of reliable witnesses? Quite lately I was honored by two statements — one made in writing, and one in language of surpassing eloquence—by gentlemen whose veracity they assure me has never been called in question excepting by a low rabble, who ought to have been hanged long ago if they had their merit. Those gentlemen seem to be equally conversant with the value of sheep and pure Bible education, green crops and Popery, while they know every turn of a peasant's mind, and can read his motives better than he can himself. Would you have me insensible to the advantage of possessing such a mine of information?"

Lord Wallingford, seeing the smile which played on Mr. Bentley's face, joined with the quiet sarcasm of his words, found that he was one not likely to be turned from the path of rectitude, and that the cause of the long-suffering people would be safe in his hands. Smiling, he said: "I see, Mr. Bentley, you are a man of penetration. Have you seen Margin, the agent, yet?"

"Why, my lord, he did me the honor of introducing himself this morning, after my arrival. He is the gentleman to whose moving eloquence I alluded just now, and from whose inexhaustible mine of information I expect such valuable aids to the acquisition of wealth."

"And he really had the effrontery to look an honest man in the face? Your allusion to mines, in connection with his name, is more apropos than you are aware of. Did you know that he had a lawsuit with me, Mr. Bentley, respecting the mines of Cooldnure?"

"No, my lord; but I shall consider myself your lordship's debtor if you will kindly inform me of the transaction."

Here Lord Wallingford entered into the details we have already laid before our readers of Jacob Margin's antecedents, and drew a faithful picture of the rascal's character, and the transformation effected on the Glengoulah estates since he became agent. Mr. Bentley's open smile vanished, and a dark cloud of indignation overspread his manly countenance, as Lord Wallingford proceeded with his narrative.

"I thank you most heartily, my lord, for this information; it shall not be lost upon me. Do you know a man named O'Hara, who lives in this neighborhood—Jeremiah O'Hara? I believe he is lame."

"Oh, yes; 'Lame Jerry' they call him—an honest, outspoken poor man he was when I left home, and a genius in his way."

"A man of surprising information for a peasant. I had a long interview with him yesterday, and he really gave me more insight into the state of affairs in Glengoulah than any one I spoke with until I had the good fortune to meet your lordship. You will, I trust, pardon the comparison."

"Pardon! my good friend; you do me quite an honor. Why, 'Lame Jerry' is one of the natural curiosities of the County Wicklow; and a tourist might as well leave the country without seeing St. Kevin's bed, or

'Glendalough, whose gloomy shore
Sky lark never warbled o'er,'

as without hearing the poetic legends of Lame Jer

ry; besides this, he possesses a large stock of historic lore, and a perfect knowledge of the condition of landlord and tenant in nearly all the countries of Europe. Jerry is the oracle of at least three counties. He lost a leg at Waterloo, for which he receives a small pension from Government."

"Ah! I see you are not aware, my lord, that he has been deprived of that trifle."

"No! Mr. Bentley! you are not serious?"

"Yes, indeed! The poor man assured me he had been describing to a number of peasantry one evening, sitting in a group on the road-side, the condition of the Russian serfs, and its vast superiority over their own, when he discovered that the Scotch steward had been playing eavesdropper. Shortly after this Margin trumped up some charge against him of conspiracy, or some other folly, and the poor man's pension was withdrawn, the learned judge assuring him he was very leniently dealt with in consequence of having but one leg."

"Oh! shame, shame! However, Jerry shall never need their pension while I live."

"He does not need it now, my lord. He tells me he wants for nothing, and never knew before how many friends he could count upon."

"Well, Mr. Bentley, that single transaction contains a volume for a man possessed of your high principles; but of this more hereafter. I hope to see you soon at Clonmalure. If you are an admirer of the picturesque, we have some handsome scenery there; if your taste lies in literary pursuits, I have a few rare books and manuscripts in my library; and if you are anything of a sportsman, I think we can please you; for my old huntsman, Larry McQuade (a perfect genius, by the way, to whom I must introduce you) boasts that he has the finest horses and dogs in the country. I expect a few friends to dinner on Tuesday, and if you will do me the honor to join our little party *sans ceremonie* I shall be most happy."

"I hope your lordship will be so good as to hold me excused. I am sincerely thankful for your kindness, but I purpose leaving Ireland in a few days, and prefer remaining quiet until my plans are more matured. I merely came this time to have ocular demonstration of convictions already established in my mind. I purpose returning in May, and then, my lord, I hope we shall spend many happy hours together."

The gentlemen shook hands and parted, mutually pleased with the frank and genial qualities they discovered in each other.

Mr. Bentley wrote Margin from England to notify the tenants that he would not require the March rent to be paid until the third week of May, and that they should then meet him at Glengoulah Castle, as he intended giving them a collation on the lawn, thus introducing himself to all of them in person. He also invited Margin, Sandy M'Glauren, and all the bailiffs, Bible readers, etc., etc., formerly in the employ of his predecessor.

Margin sent the notification around only on the eve of rent-day. He never performed a more distasteful task, and put it off until the last moment.

The invitation augered well, and high hopes began once more to take possession of hearts where only despair had so long dwelt. Still the people felt a little disappointed that Margin was retained as agent, but consoled themselves with the hope that he would be at least shorn of the power to do evil any more.

15*

CHAPTER XXX.

May came at last, and with the daisies and primroses came the summons to the landlord's entertainment. The castle and lawn presented a gay appearance. An immense marquee was erected, underneath which long tables were spread, covered with substantials of every variety. Pipers and fiddlers, in the midst of groups, were dispersed through the tent and lawn; but the chair of honor was reserved for Darby Wholahan. It was an old-fashioned high-backed chair, placed on an elevation, festooned with evergreens and flowers, and was arranged at the head of the tent under a clump of larch-trees that trailed their graceful branches like a bower on either side of him, and where all could see him when the canvas was rolled up.

When the repast was finished, Mr. Bentley, accompanied by Mr. De Courcy, entered the tent, and was introduced to the tenantry by their old and loved agent. Baskets of wine were opened on all sides, and landlord, tenants and all drank health, long-life and happiness to each other in flowing bumpers. A party of gentlemen from the surrounding and neighboring county came in, including Sir Lawrence O'Donnell and Lord Wallingford, and pleasant greetings were exchanged. To Toney Byrne, whom the neighbors had placed at the head of the centre-table —in spite of all his entreaties—they paid special attention. Mr. Bentley jumped lightly on a bench and addressed the people:

"Men of Glengoulah: I invited you here to-day for a threefold purpose. First, that we might all become acquainted with each other; secondly, that I might try to do justice where so much necessity for it existed; and thirdly, that I would see you enjoy yourselves. We Englishmen are said to be very gruff fellows; but I beg to assure you that I am a very sociable character, not at all long-faced, but on the contrary a great admirer of rational amusements, and a believer in the old adage that 'God loves a cheerful heart.' You see, though a very modest man, I can sound my own praises. I feel confident when we become better acquainted we shall feel for each other that esteem and affection which should exist between a good landlord and worthy tenantry, somewhat resembling the ties of mutual love and respect existing between a father and his children. I have English tenantry too, to whom I am much attached; but as I have not the gift of ubiquity, I have decided upon residing every alternate year in Ireland and England. Having said so much by way of introducing myself, I shall now refer to my second object in calling you around me.

"Men of Glengoulah, I have made the most minute investigations in your regard, and am quite satisfied you have been a maligned and misrepresented people. You have suffered much for some years past, and it is but fair to reward those who merit it. To all my tenantry I give an abatement of twenty-five per cent.; to some, who have been more especially imposed upon, and whose cases will receive immediate attention, a further abatement will be made." (A burst of cheers rang through hill and dale.) "Anthony Byrne, I beg to inform you that you shall be fully reinstated in your old farm, which shall be newly stocked, to compensate you in some small degree for the injustice you suffered and bore so admirably. Any alterations you deem necessary in the new house, which was erected after the fire, shall be made at my expense. For your eldest son, who is now old enough to do for himself, I have a choice farm; and for your daughter—the widow of poor Dempsey—I have ordered an annuity to be settled upon her and her heirs forever." Cheer after cheer broke forth, and the old hills gave back the echoes oft renewed. Toney Byrne stood up and made vain efforts to speak; but the tears which coursed down his cheeks were more eloquent than words. Mr. Bentley resumed: "These are only acts of simple justice, my friends, and not worth thanking for. Every injustice on my estates shall be repaired. Mr. Margin will please come forward. Jacob Margin, I arraign you before the tribunal of a people whose sacred rights you have trampled upon, whose holiest feelings you have outraged, whose homes you have made desolate or levelled with the dust."

"I was but the servant of your right reverend relation, Mr. Bentley. I only followed my orders!" exclaimed Margin, sneeringly.

"Peace, man! I know your antecedents. You had sent your victims to the penal colony, and to the gallows, before you laid eyes on the Glengoulah estates. I do not seek to justify the memory of my unfortunate predecessor; but I know who was his evil counsellor and his willing tool. In the presence of the people I dismiss you in disgrace. You are no longer agent of mine. I also dismiss your colleague, Sandy McGlauren, and all your troop of cormorants, bailiffs, Bible-readers, and the rest.

You, Margin, are an old man, and I advise you to repent of your misdeeds and make restitution."

Margin quickly disappeared. Silence reigned for a few moments. Though brimful of joy at the announcement, no voice was raised in triumph. With that instinctive delicacy which is pre-eminently the characteristic of the Irish people, they refrained from rejoicing over a fallen foe. Mr. Bentley resumed: "I have the happiness to announce to you that Mr. De Courcy"—at the mention of that honored name all sprang to their feet, and cheer after cheer echoed and re-echoed through the hills—"Mr. De Courcy, who loves you all as his children." Again the wild cheers broke forth, and the people seemed perfectly crazy. Mr. Bentley, laughing, said: "I see I cannot name that name. Well, a certain gentleman has resigned his seat in Parliament, where he long and vainly strove to obtain a fair settlement of the landlord and tenant question, and prefers again to become a quiet country gentleman, living at peace amongst those who love him, and ——" Here his voice was drowned in cheers and shouts from several parties.

"God bless him, and you too, Mr. Bentley!" "Long life to ye both!" "That you may never die at all!"

"I see you are not willing to listen to me."

A stentorian voice shouted: "Boys, give three rale Irish cheers and a *cead mille failtha* for Mr. Bentley, our good landlord!" These were given with a hearty good will, throwing up of hats, and the wildest enthusiasm.

"Now boys," cried the same voice, "hould your tongues. Not another word. Let the gentleman spake."

"I often heard," resumed Mr. Bentley, "of an Irish cheer; but now I understand what it is."

"I have not much more to say. Mr. De Courcy has done me a great favor in accepting the agency of these estates. It is to him a labor of love, he says, and I know you will all appreciate his kindness in saying so. He is not only my agent, but my most valued and honored friend. The property shall be entirely controlled by his wise head, who knows the necessities and capacities of the tenantry. I now want to see you enjoy yourselves in dancing, and all your national pastimes."

There were loud calls for Mr. De Courcy, but he merely bowed and smiled his acknowledgments, while they drank his health and rent the air with cheers. When he retired, Lame Jerry arose and begged "before the dancing commenced, that every one should fill their glasses and drink long life and every prosperity and happiness to their respected neighbor and loved friend, Anthony O'Byrne, the old chieftain of Glengoulah." Again the old hills gave back the echo of the oft-renewed cheers which seemed never-ending, when Darby Wholahan jumped up, rolling his sightless eyes around, exclaiming:

"Boys, I'm going to improvise." [Cries of "Bravo, Darby! it's yourself can do it!"] "I am going, I say, to improvise. Most of yees knows what that manes; but, lest there should be any gorsoons whose powers of discrimination are not nately developed, I'll translate it for their edification. I said, I was going to improvise. Now that manes, my young friends, I'm going to compose a song for this truly festive occasion, illustrative of the bards of old in the ancient halls of our forefathers. I shall also improvise an air upon my ancient instrument—the pipes." ["Bravo! Long life to Darby Wholahan, the king of pipers; the best musician in the barony! aye, or in the whole county, for that matter!"]

Darby sat down and flourished a number of chords with great rapidity, then struck a particular key; and gazing upward, as if reviewing the past, present and future in the light of the soul, he broke forth in a wild but most harmonious recitative of the ancient glories of " Green Erin of the Streams "—her ages of martyrdom and long-sufferings for the faith of Christ, the valiant deeds of her sons, foremost among whom was the gallant O'Byrne of Glengoulah. He then touched on the penal laws, their disinheriting effects and consequent impoverishment of the old Celtic race, shoving them out by wholesale and introducing in their stead the Sassenach, some of whom were as bad as the evil one could make them, but whose wicked deeds we would pass over to-day in honor of him who would become "more Irish than the Irish themselves," and under whose benign sway the lovely hills and vales of their country, so celebrated in song and story, would again resound with the joyous laugh and merry dance—where the poor and the stranger would ever find a welcome, and the bard be honored as in days of yore!

He ceased. During the recitative a number of gentlemen from the castle stole on tip-toe, one by one, into the tent, and listened delightedly. Now cheers, bravos and compliments flowed in upon all sides. Mr. Bentley and many other gentlemen came forward as he ceased, to shake by the hand a bard who combined poet and musician in his own person. Mr. Bentley requested " that Mr. Wholahan would call and see him at the castle on his next visit to Glengoulah. By that time he expected Mrs. Bentley and his family there, and as his wife was somewhat of a musician herself, she would be pleased to meet a genius like Mr. Wholahan," etc. A proud and happy man was Darby that night. Such tones as he brought out of the pipes were never before heard by mortal ears. As our droll friend Tom Moody said: "It would make a cat spake to see the humors of the ould head joggin' from side to side, now smilin' down at the pipes, and then snuffin' up at the stars."

It was indeed a most entrancing sight. The sun had sunk behind the western hills, but the sapphire and golden tints which accompanied his declining course were still spread far over the firmament, while the moon, sailing slowly and majestically onward, threw a flood of silver radiance on the old woods skirting the noble lawn, and shed a trail of glittering spangles on the bosom of the Ovoca. Groups of happy boys and girls footed away right merrily "The Rocky Road to Dublin," "Lather the Wig," "Trip to the Cottage," etc., on the smooth velvet turf. Occasionally Darby's voice could be heard: "That's yourself, Mick; but it's no wonder you do it so nately with such a partner! Sure, Bessie

Daily wouldn't hurt a bunch of primroses if she danced on them, her step is so light. Ah, Bessie, you decavin' rogue! though you tread so lightly on the turf, upon my conscience you're hard enough upon the boys' hearts!" "Why, then, Mrs. Fogarty! is that your voice I hear; and is it only looking on you are—you that could bate seven baronies at the dance?" "Bedad, it's the truth you're spakin', Mr. Wholahan. Come out here, Mrs. Fogarty, and let us show these youngsters what dancin' was in our day. Oh, by the powers of Moll Kelley, I'll take no excuse. Sure, it's many a time we danced together before either of us was married, and I'll be bound we have the old kick in our foot yet. What's your favorite, ma'am? Bedad, you must have it! Darby, give us 'The New Married Bride!' and now clear the road, boys?"

Such were the scenes of merriment all around. Between ten and eleven o'clock they began to wend their way homeward, with bounding steps and gleesome jokes, betokening hearts awaking to a sense of happiness and contentment.

CONCLUSION.

ANOTHER year flew by, and once more the vines and flowers in her old home were tended by the careful hand of Winnie. The children played among the flower-beds in front of the handsome, capacious cottage erected by the late Bishop Biggs for Sandy McGlauren.

Retribution had at last overtaken the whole troop of vampires. The same day that Toney Byrne took possession of his old farm, the soul of Jacob Margin was brought before the bar of Eternal Justice. He died of putrid fever after seven days' sickness, at his residence, Fawnbrook Lodge. Three days afterward a stately hearse, with nodding plumes, and half a dozen carriages, accompanied his remains to the Protestant church-yard of Ardmore. A few miserable outcasts, whom his tyranny had made desperate, flung stones at the hearse and cursed the senseless clay as it passed along; but the majority of the people shook their heads in horror, and, getting out of the way, crossed themselves, and invoked a prayer to be delivered from the evil one. Such was the end of Jacob Margin. It was said not even one of his own relatives ever shed a tear for him. He went to his grave "unwept, unpitied," and but too well known.

Sandy McGlauren went back to Scotland, a richer if not a wiser man; while Faulkner, the Bible-reader, and his *confreres*, betook themselves to "White Friar's Hall," to shout for Thresham Gregg and the Dublin Corporation.

Mr. De Courcy, when he had the affairs of the estate restored to their former order, and saw the people once more contented and happy, took with his family a tour on the continent, which he had long contemplated. About six months after his departure little Mary Dempsey came home from school earlier than usual one day, and throwing her arms around the neck of her grandfather, with whom she was a great pet, exclaimed: "Oh, grandaddy! I have the greatest news for you! We were all dismissed from school to-day at twelve o'clock. First, we were brought to the chapel to join in a *Te Deum* that all the nuns sang in thanksgiving to God. Sister Norah played the organ; but she could not sing: her voice was choked with sobs. She told me to tell you in particular the news she had heard. Now what will you give me if I tell you?" and the young rogue peered laughingly into his face. Her grandfather fondled the little prattler and stroked her fair curls. Then he said:

"I wont give anything. I don't care to hear it!"

"Yes, you do, you bad old grandaddy! You'd give ever so much to hear it!"

"Well, I'll give you a kiss."

"Oh, I'll get plenty of them without telling anything."

"Well, then, I'll buy you a pretty picture the next time I go to Ardmore."

"Will you, for sure and certain?"

"For sure and certain."

"Then I'll tell you. Sister Norah got a letter from Rome this morning, from her father, telling her he had become a Catholic; and on the same day and in the same church our own Mr. De Courcy and all his family were baptized, and all made their first communion. Now, grandfather, isn't that good news?"

Toney Byrne did not utter a word—he raised his hands and eyes to heaven, and going into his room knelt down. The child saw the large tears streaming down his cheeks, and she ran off to find her mother and grandmother and communicate the joyful intelligence. Soon it was over the whole country, and from every hill-top that night bonfires blazed and groups danced merrily around them. Every old flute and fiddle ever scratched was brought forth and put in requisition for the dance, and when all instruments failed the best whistler or jigger took up the tune and footed it with right good will until the near approach of midnight.

On any Sunday morning early, long before the chapel-bell of Tinmanogue gives warning that the holy mass will soon commence, if you chance to be passing and peer through the sweet-briar hedge among the peaceful graves, you will not fail to see a pensive woman of prepossessing appearance, dressed in plain black, surrounded by a group of hushed children, kneeling around a grave which she frequently stoops to kiss and bedew with her tears.

And "Aft in the simmer eve's gloamin'" the same figure may be observed (attended by one or other of her children, and sometimes by an old man) plucking the withered leaves from the rose bushes which hang lovingly over the cross at the head of the grave, or carefully removing the weeds from the well-kept turf studded with daisies. Would you know who sleeps beneath? Then read the inscription on the white marble slab inserted into the chapel wall above the grave:

BRYAN DEMPSEY,
DEPARTED IN THE PEACE OF THE LORD,
February 13th, 1846,
Aged 28 years.
REQUIESCAT IN PACE.
"Glengoulah forever mourns her youthful martyr!"

Watch the movements of this mourner a little longer and you will see her proceed to another grave, upon which she bestows equal care, and fervently kisses the green sod, praying all the while.

A box tomb of Carrara marble stands at the head of this grave. On the top of the tomb two angels, finely carved, hold between them an immortal crown, and seem already on the wing for realms of bliss.

The inscription reads thus:

ERECTED BY HIS SORROWING PARISHIONERS,
TO THE MEMORY OF
REV. EUGENE PATRICK ESMOND,
FOR FIFTY-SIX YEARS
FATHER, FRIEND, COUNSELLOR, AND PASTOR OF GLENGOULAH,
Died a Martyr to Charity, February 20th, 1846, Aged 98 Years.
Requiescat in Pace.

These graves and her children are the great charge of Winnie's life. The white marble slab over Bryan was the gift of Clara Menville, through Mr. De Courcy, who carried out her wishes when she entered the convent.

Winnie's life glided peacefully on with her father and mother. Many of the old people have dropped to sleep in the hope of a glorious resurrection, but Toney Byrne yet lives, loved and respected by all who know him.

Still on winter evenings the neighbors gather around his fireside as in days of yore, and beguile the hours with legend, and song, and tale. Still Toney watches the budding corn and waving fields he tilled for so many years, and his life is a continual prayer of thanksgiving. He thinks of the old neighbors who were persecuted to death or forced to emigrate to foreign lands, while he can sit securely and smoke at his porch, listening to the concert the sweet birds are making; and in the humility of his heart he wonders why it is that God has so especially favored him. The terrible trials he has passed through have faded from his memory; or if ever spoken of, he always says.

"Well, don't you see how God in his tender mercies brought us through all? And now we're better off than ever! Praises be to His holy name!"

And now, dear reader, lest in this changeful world some new evil should befall us, I will make my adieu, hoping you will follow the advice I gave you in the first chapter—to visit before you die the lovely hills and vales, not of Wicklow alone, but of "Erin the beautiful."

If you have not the good fortune to see Anthony Byrne in the flesh, you will, thank God, see many, many left in that grand old land with the spirit and the virtue of the Chieftain of Glengoulah.

THE END.

www.ingramcontent.com/pod-product-compliance
Lightning Source LLC
Chambersburg PA
CBHW031422230426
43668CB00007B/399